PRI

PRIMO

The Story of 'Man Mountain' Carnera

Frederic Mullally

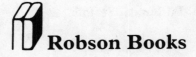
Robson Books

First published in paperback in Great Britain in 1999
by Robson Books, 10 Blenheim Court, Brewery Road,
London N7 9NT

First published in hardback in 1991 by Robson Books
Ltd.

Copyright © 1991 Frederic Mullally
The right of Frederic Mullally to be identified as author
of this work has been asserted by him in accordance
with the Copyright, Designs and Patents Act 1988

British Library Cataloguing in Publication Data
A catalogue record for this title is available from the
British Library

ISBN 1 86105 242 1

Printed in Great Britain by
St. Edmundsbury Press,
Bury St. Edmunds, Suffolk

Contents

'He steps practically unchanged out of the limbo of things that used to frighten or excite us. Had he but one eye in the center of his forehead, he might pass for Cyclops. Indeed, as he climbed into the ring in Madison Square Garden he might have stepped from some nursery frieze or from between the covers of an imaginatively illustrated copy of Jack the Giant Killer ... It is from this tribe that Carnera springs.'

Paul Gallico

'Primo Carnera, the Ambling Alp, a circus strongman fashioned into a fighter, has been derided as a freak foisted on the public purely on his size. His boxing was not as crude as all that and probably a good deal better than Jess Willard's, the other six-and-a-half-foot champion. The tragedy of Carnera lies not in his lack of craft but his exploitation by unscrupulous managers, who left him without a cent and forced him into wrestling, where at length he made a good living.'

Harry Carpenter

1
A Sad Night for Italy

To start with, he shouldn't have been an Italian, facing a popular white American with a mandate to restore the title to the USA that night of 14 June 1934 in the Madison Square Garden Bowl. He should not have been deprived in his corner of the critical support of Big Bill Duffy. He should not have been caught off-balance in that first round by a looping right from Max Baer and fallen so clumsily as to rip those tendons in his right ankle and leg. He should have protested, as Bill Duffy certainly would have, at the repeated and strength-sapping low punches and hooks to the kidneys. Above all, he should not have been made the object, from the beginning of the bout, of such contemptuous buffoonery by the Californian Jew. He, Primo Carnera, was the heavyweight champion of the world, only the second non-American to be wearing the crown and the only Italian boxer ever to have fought for it. He deserved some respect.

But nothing seemed to be going right. There was a sea of about 50,000 people filling the great outdoor arena on Long Island and they were easily out-yelling his compatriots, most of whom were concentrated in the cheaper seats around the outer rim of the Bowl. Bill Duffy and Owney Madden, his American managers, were both in jail, leaving only Luigi Soresi and Billy Defoe in the champ's corner. Billy was fine, but he was being elbowed out that night by – huh – the vice-president of the New

York branch of the Banca Commerciale Italiana, who knew as much about the fight game as the little trainer knew about stock options. All Soresi kept saying, in Italian, was, 'Take no notice of the clowning. Just watch out for his right.'

The punches he could handle, over the first four rounds, anyway. He had already been floored twice in the first round, three times (locked with his opponent) in the second and once in the third. What those wildly cheering idiots out there failed to understand was, the blows had not hurt. Each time, he had been up at once without a count and had fought right on, ignoring the pain in his ankle. What *did* hurt were the guffaws from the ringside seats when Baer, entangled with him on the canvas, tickled him under the arm with his glove and cried, 'Last one up's a sissy!' Oh, he knew how to upset him, that *maledetto* playboy. Like, during the physical in the Boxing Commission office prior to the fight when, with the press looking on, he pretended to pluck hairs from the champ's bare chest while intoning, 'He loves me, he loves me not . . .' How would joker Maxie have liked it if the bout had been held in Italy, with Carnera making hurtful remarks in slangy Italian and no way for him to crack back?

These unprofessional antics, it was dirty, as dirty in its own way as the punch Baer had slammed at him in the third round while he was only halfway to his feet, with one knee still on the canvas, and not even a caution from the referee. If Duffy had been at the ringside, Arthur Donovan would have heard from him. He would have been told what was going to happen to *him*, after the fight, if he ignored any more fouls by Baer. And Donovan would have got the message pretty damn quick, for when Duffy speaks you are also hearing the voice of Owney ('The Killer') Madden. But neither of them was there at the ringside that night to watch him retain his beautiful title, which he was certain he would do. And fox-face Soresi, who had bought into the management syndicate, was only interested in getting his paws on the champ's purse which, win or lose, would be somewhere around $130,000. What did Luigi care about Baer's roars of laughter when his feints came off; his kiss-blowing at the ringside beauties; his ploy of turning his back and strolling away, then turning back to the champ and crying out in mock distress, 'Oh, dear! It's a crude fellow actually attacking me!' To Soresi, this was the kind of stuff the fight fans were expecting for their money – and of course the prospect of seeing the world title back where it really belonged, in the good old USA.

Well, they could forget about that bit. Mind you, Baer was going to be no pushover. He was big: 6ft 2½ in. tall and weighing in at 210 pounds. At 25 years of age, he had scored twenty-nine knockouts in the course of forty-six bouts, and ten wins on points. But he was up against a really big fella this time: over three in. taller and heavier by 53 lb of muscle and sinew, with a record of sixty-one knockouts over the six years he had been fighting, which was just a year longer than Baer's career in the ring. Trouble was, Baer had clearly profited greatly and dangerously from what he had learned just a few months back during the filming of *The Prizefighter and the Lady* in MGM's Hollywood studios. He and Carnera had both been cast for the movie, but the champ had wanted to pull out of the deal when they told him the script called for him to end up, after nine rounds, being flattened by Max Baer. It didn't make sense. Besides, what would his compatriots back in Italy think? And il Duce, Benito Mussolini, who had received him with an embrace last October in the Palazzo Venezia?

Soresi had persuaded him to go along with the script. The lady of the film's title was the great and beautiful movie star, Myrna Loy, and the truth was that Baer, with his dark curly hair, dimples and radiant smile, was more in the Hollywood image of a romantic idol than the world heavyweight champion could ever be. It was only a film after all; everyone would know that. And the $5,000 on offer, for just a few days' work, would more than cover those breach of promise damages awarded in London in favour of that damn girl. So he had played the role, and everyone who had seen the edited movie had raved about the realism of the fight scenes, in which Baer wins the first round, Carnera the next seven, and Baer the wild and exciting last two rounds. Baer had been paid far less for his part in the film, but he had jumped at the offer. He was already a contender for Carnera's heavyweight crown. In the course of those fast and furious rounds they had fought for the cameras – the equivalent of about thirty rounds in all – he had been able to analyse the real-life champ's strengths and weaknesses far more shrewdly than he ever could have done by watching from the ringside or on a screen projection. He soon learned that Carnera had inadequate defence against a looping right-hand swing to the jaw. And it was a lesson Baer had already applied to useful effect in each of the past four rounds of this fifteen-round title fight. During the filming he had had to pull these particular punches, and Carnera could ride any that might have connected by moving his weight back off the left foot and on to the right. He was still doing that, instinctively, here in the Bowl, but that damned ankle was thwarting the reflex, either by slowing it or actually giving way and putting him off balance.

Round 5:
Carnera, limping, begins with a body attack followed by a left hook to the jaw. Baer connects with a right-hand kidney punch followed by a two-fisted body attack. The champion boxes his way out of it before landing a left hook to Baer's jaw but missing with a right. Baer's hard right to the jaw causes Carnera to hold. They break and the contender sends over a haymaker of a right that breaks the champ's nose. As the blood spurts freely, Baer bursts out laughing and lands another right, smack on the nose. Now Carnera, roaring with anger, fights back and drives Baer into his own corner for the first time. A wild right to the jaw shakes the champ, who enfolds his opponent in both arms as the bell signals the end of the round.

Max Albert Baer was born in Omaha, Nebraska, of a German–Jewish father and a Scots–Irish mother. His parents moved later to Livermore, California, where Baer Snr set himself up as a wholesale butcher. Max lacked style and was no ring technician, but he could hit hard, especially with his right hand, take punishment, and his chunky good looks and sunny nature had won him a growing *afición* among fight enthusiasts and the press during his five-year climb through the heavyweight ranks to the status of contender. His Greek god's body, together with the cavalier treatment of opponents in the ring, made him irresistible to a certain class of bloodlusting female ringsiders, who fought among themselves for the privilege of draining his unspent energy after a fight. But for all his bouncy good nature and self-indulgent clowning, the killer instinct could be counted upon to break out, snarling, if he thought he had an opponent ready for slaughter. And slaughter it had been in the San Francisco ballpark on 25 August 1930 when, in the second round of a bout, the heavyweight Frankie Campbell made the mistake of turning his back on Baer, believing he was down for a short count, and walking to a neutral corner as the rules required. Baer, up almost at once, sprang after his opponent and smashed a right at his jaw as he turned around, arms down. Campbell, who had been scoring up to then by superior skill, never fully recovered from the blow. He managed to keep on his feet until the fifth round, when Baer unleashed a two-fisted barrage of hooks and swings long past the stage when the referee should have intervened and stopped the fight. Campbell collapsed, was taken in a coma to hospital and died within hours from brain damage. It brought a year's suspension for Baer from the California Boxing Commission, but did his reputation no harm whatever among the bimbos and poolroom *conoscenti*.

Over the next two years, Baer won fourteen bouts against ranking heavyweights, eight times by knockouts, and lost only three. And in June 1933 he had won his right to a bid for the title with a technical knockout of the 1930–32 world champion, the German Max Schmeling, but only after being repeatedly warned for low punching, warnings he was able to disregard as a Jew fighting a German in New York in the year of the Nazi Party's rise to power.

One year later, ringside commentaries on the Carnera–Baer title fight were being clearly heard over short-wave throughout Italy. Benito Mussolini was unable to listen in, being totally absorbed in his first meeting with fellow-dictator Adolf Hitler in Venice, just a hundred miles or so away from the champion's birthplace in the little village of Sequals.

Round 6:
The bell sounds. The seconds duck out of the ring. But what's this? Instead of coming out fighting, Baer waltzes around the gaping Carnera with a flip 'Pardon, Signore – I'll be right back,' pauses in the champion's corner long enough to work the soles of his shoes in the dry resin while he grins over his shoulder. He then turns around and squares up. They trade punches, Carnera using straight lefts to the face and body, Baer responding with both fists, but not connecting solidly with his right until towards the end of the round. As in round 4, the giant Italian is out-boxing and scoring over the Californian who, between brief toe-to-toe exchanges, taunts his opponent with little jigs and exaggerated grimaces. At the bell, Baer struts to his corner like a peacock.

Carnera never for a moment doubted that the title would still be his at the end of the fight. Baer was hitting him hard but he could take it and was giving back as good as he got. His footwork – usually a wonder to spectators in a pugilist of his size – was becoming more like a shuffle, thanks to the leg injury and the draining effect of low blows and kidney punches, but the strength was still there in his shoulders and arms and in his resolve now to punish Max Baer for his outlandish behaviour. This was happening in front of no fewer than five former heavyweight champions of the world, one of the largest group of boxing's greats ever assembled on such an occasion. He could look right there into the press section at Jack Dempsey, Gene Tunney and at the man from whom he had wrested the title just a year ago in this very arena. Further back was Tommy Burns and at the further fringe of the ringside seats sat none other than Jack Johnson, who had held the title from 1908 to 1915. They had all been heroes to him, and he had now achieved equality in status with them, worldwide, only to be made a laughing-stock by this capering Californian playboy. While Billy sponged him, Luigi

RACHEL BUTLER   PHYSIO   8-30

0845 1222 526   5-5-09

LELT

07786621791   BiLLy P.

£7·43   MON 8-6-09   £5·79

was telling him in rapid Italian to ignore his opponent's bad manners and to keep piling up points with his left. But he was going to do more than that: he was going to find an opening for a right-hand slam that would put Baer on his back for the count, thereby ridiculing the Manhattan bookmakers for making the contender favourite for the big fight at 7 to 5 on. And if there should be any more falls caused by that *maledetto* ankle, he would continue to reject Billy's advice to take a count of seven or eight, but would again be up on his feet at once, proving to the thousands of fellow-Italians who had travelled to the Bowl from all over the USA that he had not been hurt by Baer.

Rounds 7, 8 and 9:
The champion is on the attack throughout all three rounds, repeatedly scoring with long and short lefts and with right hooks and uppercuts. He now has Baer's own dangerous right under defensive control and the challenger is thrown back on foul punches and clowning, provoking an angry protest from Carnera which the referee ignores. Baer is now making a practice of giving his corner a reassuring wink whenever the champ connects, and if he is tiring he makes it appear so more out of boredom than punishment. Meanwhile, Carnera – at one point angrily calling on Baer to fight – is establishing a clear points lead.

It was agonizing. It was as if his leg, from the knee down, was caught in a vice that tightened itself cruelly any time it took even a fraction of his weight. There were still six rounds to go, unless he could put Baer out before then or win with a technical knockout. A points win over the distance would be no disgrace against a contender as big and tough as this one, but tonight was the third time he had defended his title and it had been a points win against Paolino Uzcudun in Rome the previous October and then against Tommy Loughran in Miami, three and a half months before. The youngest son of *il Duce*, who had attended the Uzcudun fight with his father, had wanted to know, imperiously, why he hadn't knocked out the Basque fighter as he had dealt with most of his opponents during his career.

Soresi had moved in to explain that Carnera had dislocated the middle joint of his right-hand index finger against Uzcudun's head in the course of the fourth round. The hand was useless from then on as an offensive weapon and there was no way he could knock out a twice European heavyweight champion with his left fist. Max Baer had weighed in about 4 lb lighter than Uzcudun, but he was three inches taller and nine years younger and was showing no sign of having been hurt by the right uppercuts he had been taking from the champ during these past three rounds.

Six more rounds to go . . . there was a cable back in his dressing room from Achille Starace, Secretary of Italy's Fascist Party and the nation's next most powerful man after Mussolini. It read 'IN YOUR BOUT WITH BAER YOU WILL WIN'. It seemed more like a command than an expression of confidence. And there was the cable from Emilia, datelined London. 'MY BEST WISHES FOR YOUR VICTORY TONIGHT'. She should care whether he won or lost. Her lawyers had already slapped a lien on his purse money from tonight's fight. What with that debt and the money he owed three of his managers, the tax people, his tailor and the Hotel Victoria, there would not be much left to add to the couple of thousand dollars that was all he had to show for six years' prize-fighting around the world. But he had the Title, the greatest gift that Sport could bestow upon any athlete. His place in history was assured.

Round Ten:
Carnera comes out confidently and responds with clubbing lefts and rights to Baer's renewed low punches. They slug it out for most of the round until a hard right from the now unsmiling Californian lands on the champion's jaw, visibly staggering him. Baer is momentarily stopped by Referee Donovan from following up. At the signal, 'Fight on!' the champion is hit by a combination of lefts and right to the jaw and goes down. As he starts up at the count of four, he sees Soresi about to throw in the towel and snarls, in Italian, 'Do that and I'll kill you!' The bell

rings just as he gets to his feet.

Round Eleven:
Seemingly fully recovered, Carnera launches a furious attack until he is floored by a tremendous right. Up at a count of two, he scores with rights to Baer's jaw but is dropped again, only to stagger up at the count of three despite Billy Defoe's yelling to him to 'Take it to eight!' He cannot hear and possibly cannot even see straight. Donovan waves Baer back and stops the fight. It is a technical knockout, two minutes and sixteen seconds into the round.

The ex-champion limped back to his corner with tears running down his face, and he spent the next three weeks with his ankle in plaster while the torn ligaments mended. Max Baer declared that he would be willing to give Carnera a return match in September 'if there is enough public interest'.

In northern Italy, the ex-champ's father, Sante Carnera, quietly stole away from the village of Sequals and took refuge in the town of Fanna where, according to his wife Giovanna, he expected to remain until comment on the fight is 'less excruciating'.

2
'Will I have Enough to Eat?'

Léon Sée was born in 1877 in the city of Lille in northern France. By the turn of the century his father, a well-to-do businessman, had abandoned hope of his son's joining the family firm. The lad had three main interests: philosophy, journalism and the sport of boxing. He read and graduated in philosophy at college; journalism would come later. In the meanwhile he spent his weekends and holidays training for his début as an amateur in the gentle art of self-defence. This would have to be across the Channel in Britain, where men fought only with their fists, rather than with fists and feet in the *savate* style of *la boxe française*. Fortunately, his father had both business and family connections in Birmingham, and through these the 17-year-old Léon was able to compete in the Midlands amateur boxing championships in the only class open to one of his slight physique: the bantam-weight. His enthusiasm for the sport was not matched however by any natural skills and, after having, as he put it later, 'the shit knocked out of me' by a succession of hardy Midlanders, he decided to indulge his passion for boxing from the outside rather than the inside of the ring. It was a great game so long as you were not on the receiving end of the punishment: this was the lesson of his début in Birmingham. It was also the seed that would grow into Léon Sée's 'Great Idea'.

Over the next thirty-four years, Sée probably did more than any other single person to introduce Queensberry rules boxing, amateur and professional, to France. He published and edited the magazine *La Boxe et les Boxeurs*, founded the periodical *La Culture Physique* and the daily *Les Nouvelles Sportives* and wrote about boxing for several leading French newspapers. At the same time, he started up the Féderation Française de Boxe and set himself up as a manager and promoter with a training camp at Saint-Germain-en-Laye, to the west of Paris. By 1928, the little man with the Groucho eyebrows and pre-Hitler moustache had managed scores of boxers and guided nine of them to French championships. It was in the summer of that year that Sée received a letter from one of his former pupils, an ex-heavyweight champion of France named Paul Journée.

Upon retiring from the ring, Journée had set up a gymnasium in his home town of Arcachon, a seaside resort near Bordeaux, where he earned a modest living training young aspirants to the title he had once held. He usually took time out, whenever a travelling circus or fair hit town, to look in at the boxing or wrestling booths. One never knew: there might be a one-time opponent of his, down on his luck and challenging the beefy young locals to go a couple of rounds with him for 1,000 francs if they finished on their feet. It would be *drôle* to see the expression on such a veteran's face as Paul Journée made a show of climbing into the ring.

There were no former professionals working the booth on the evening of 15 March 1928. Instead there was a young giant in torn shorts and frayed rope sandals who managed by brute strength alone to overcome whoever accepted his challenge to wrestle, box or lift weights. He was billed as 'Juan the Unbeatable Spaniard', but before leaving the fairground Journée learned that the invincible Spaniard was in fact a 21-year-old Italian named Primo Carnera. He had been with the travelling 'Sporting Ring' for almost three years and customarily took on up to ten challengers a day for a pittance of a wage. He slept on straw in one of the wagons, without changing clothes, and had only recently spent two weeks in hospital after passing out from undernourishment. Journée scribbled a note, inviting Carnera to meet him next day away from the fairground.

★

Primo Carnera was almost nine years old when Italy declared war on its northern neighbour Austria at midnight on 23 May 1915, thereby joining Britain, France and Russia in the war against the Triple Alliance of Germany and Austria–Hungary. Carnera's native village of Sequals lay within the province of Pordenone which fell to the advancing Austro-German forces in 1917. The Carneras were of Alpine stock, originally settled in a Trentino village close to the Austrian frontier. Around the year AD 1000, a branch of the family moved a hundred miles east to the Friuli village of Sequals, birthplace over the succeeding centuries of such talented Carneras as the sculptor Paolo, the painter Simone, the writer Bortolomeo and a succession of king's *cavalieri* such as Ettore Carnera and Guiseppe, Ugo, Luigi and Edoardo of that ilk.* Such data as might have been known about Primo's immediate forebears were lost with the death of his father, Sante, in 1941, but the circumstantial evidence leads to the assumption that Primo was born into a branch of the Carneras undistinguished as to talent and unfavoured by material fortune. The First World War occupation by Austro-Germany of what is now known as the Friuli–Venezia–Giulia region brought famine to the village of Sequals. Sante Carnera had been drafted into the infantry and put to work digging trenches at the front. In his absence it fell to Primo, the first-born, to forage in the fields and woods for such appeasements of hunger as edible roots and horse-chestnuts, helped by his two younger brothers. Despite this, Primo continued to grow and by the war's end in 1918 the skinny 12-year-old was already as tall as the average male adult in the village.

There had been big, taller than average men on his mother's – the Mazziol – side of the family, but none to compare in growth with Primo, who by the age of sixteen had reached a height of 6 ft 4 in. and at 19 measured 6ft 5½ in. with an unexpanded chest girth of 45 in. Six children in all were born to Giovanna, but

---

* *Primo Carnera, Campione Senza Tempo.* Edited by Robert Vattori, p. 23 (Udine, 1987).

only three, Primo, Secondo and Severino, survived childhood, and the younger brothers fell slightly short of 6 feet in their adulthood. And their children in turn, as this author discovered, are unremarkable as to height and build. Secondo and his wife Marianna had two sons, Elvio and Giovanni, both barely 6 ft tall. They live in London where Elvio, the eldest, has a mosaics business. Giovanni ('Call me John') is the merchandising director of the Jermyn Street men's shop, New & Lingwood, whose hand-made shoes can cost around £800 a pair and receive handsome tribute from Tom Wolfe in his novel, *Bonfire of the Vanities*. Severino Carnera and his wife Mary (née Cola) had a daughter Joan, born 1949, and now living with her husband, Joseph Simplicio, in Nutley, New Jersey. Her brother, John Carnera, born six years later, also lives in the United States with his wife Julie (née Williams). Both of these offspring of Primo's youngest brother, Severino, are of áverage build, as indeed are Primo's own two children: his daughter Jean (baptized Giovanna Maria) and his son Umberto, who graduated as a doctor of medicine from the University of Guadalajara, Mexico, in 1972. Both children were born in Italy during the Second World War and in 1947 joined their parents in the USA, which became their permanent home. Jean married an electrical engineer, Philip Anderson, but subsequently divorced. Umberto was known to be in practice somewhere in the United States, but has been unresponsive to all efforts by his cousins, and by the present author, to make contact.

When Carnera first burst upon the boxing scene, the over-excited press references to his height varied from 6 ft 6 in. to 6 ft. 10 in. Even today, no two authorities seem to agree about this statistic. The *Ring Record Book*, for example, gives his height as 6 ft 5¾ in. John McCallum's *The World Heavyweight Boxing Championship* gives it as 6 ft 7 in.* But an official report by Professor Ederle of the Neuro-psychiatric Clinic of Rome, after Carnera was admitted for a thorough examination, reported him

---

* Chilton Book Co., USA, 1974.

to be 6 ft 7¼ in. tall.★ It is not unusual for a person's height to
vary fractionally over a period of time, but Ederle's report was
issued in 1933, concurrently with Mr Nat Fleischer's
authoritative *Ring Record Book*. A discrepancy of 1½ in within
the space of a year seems more suggestive of Spanish
Inquisitorial practices than pituitary vagaries. Mr Elvio
Carnera takes Nat Fleischer's side. As the nephew of a famous
boxing phenomenon, Elvio would presumably have no interest
in understating his uncle's physical dimensions, but he assured
the present writer that the *Ring Record Book* had it right. 'In
1959, my wife Barbara and I spent our honeymoon in Sequals
with Uncle Primo. The *Record Book* was lying around and I
clearly remember asking him if it was accurate about his height.
He assured me it was.'

Whatever the reason for this particular discrepancy, most of
the contemporary records during Carnera's career agree on such
items as the boxer's massive chest measurement (expanded) of
54 in., his 18½ in. flexed biceps and his reach of 81¼ in., the
longest of any (gloved) heavyweight champion. The newspapers'
medical correspondents at this time took the view that Carnera's
hugeness – more remarkable, perhaps, earlier in this century
than it would be now – was caused by early-in-life increases in
the growth hormone secretion of the pituitary gland, situated in
the floor of the skull. This causes the long bones of the body to
increase abnormally up to the age at which growth normally
ceases. But it surprises nobody who ever knew Primo Carnera
that he never used his physical advantage aggressively over
peers during childhood and early youth. Interviewed in 1967 by
the Italian weekly magazine *Oggi*, the Sequals barber, Patrizio
Ferrante, recalled that his former classmate, though conscious of
his exceptional strength, never abused it. '*Era d'animo gentile.*'
('He had a kind heart.') It is also not surprising that the clumsy
overgrowing kid was continually coming a cropper in play, as
when he tumbled from a farm cart, had his leg crushed by one of

★ *Carnera, L'Uomo Piu Forte del Mondo*, by Aldo Santini. Arnold
  Mondadori Editore, Milan, 1984.

the wheels and was laid up in bed for months.

The 1918 Armistice brought little relief from poverty for the Carneras and their fellow Friulanos. There was only a slow revival of the local mosaic industry, and while Sante sought work abroad his first-born son, whose fingers were already too big for delicate mosaic work, was apprenticed to his mother's brother, Bonaventura Mazziol, a carpenter. Primo's formal education had ended at elementary third class and he could hardly read or write and spoke no Italian, only the regional Friulano dialect. But even with these handicaps, his best hope of earning a wage would be to follow his father's example and look for work outside impoverished Italy. His aunt Antonia Mazziol had married Anselmo Cecconi, who lived at Le Mans, in north-west France, and worked in the building trade. Giovanna pleaded in tears for Primo to stay at home, but when it became obvious that his mind was made up, she managed to scrape together the third-class rail fare, one way, to Le Mans. He set forth wearing one of the only two suits his father possessed, together with a shirt and a pair of sandals donated by his maternal grandmother, who happened to have the biggest pair of feet in the village.

No two versions, among those on record, agree as to the precise chronology of events between the day Carnera left his native village to the day he was approached at Arcachon by Paul Journée. His own various accounts of how he was worked by his uncle from dawn to dusk for a pittance, with never enough to eat, were never challenged but, depending on the source, his actual age on arriving at Le Mans was anything between 13 and 15, with Carnera plumping at different times for any one of the three options. Since there was no particular capital to be made by lying about this, a more likely explanation is that his fractured English, during interviews in the early part of his career, played the usual tricks with communication. Certain it is, because inscribed in his first legal contract, that it was in March 1928 that the 21-year-old made his first practical move along the rocky road to the world heavyweight championship.

Paul Journée was a big man, but he was dwarfed by the young

fellow who rose from the park bench, cap in hand, to greet him in a bass voice reverberating out of the cavernous depths of his chest. Journée, after introducing himself, wasted no time. He was prepared to take the Italian under his management, train him for a professional boxing career and in the meantime take care of his board and lodging. He produced a contract, binding for fifteen years, with a commission of 35 per cent of all earnings to the management. It was a simple enough document, but Carnera had difficulty reading it. He then relapsed into brooding silence. Interpreting this as dissatisfaction with the basic terms, Journée was about to come up with the usual *spiel* about management overheads and handouts when his companion gave voice in his accented French to his reason for hesitating.

'*Et vraiment on pourra manger à sa faim?*' ('And I really will be able to eat all I need?')

Journée reassured him about that and the contract was signed.

For the first few nights of his new life, Carnera slept on a couch at Journée's home until a bed could be found big enough to take the length and 264 lb load of his frame. Such beds were not then available in a province of France at a time when the average height of a Frenchman fell well below even six feet, but Journée, learning that his protégé had worked in a carpenter's shop before joining the fair, took him around to a local builder who gave him a day job at three francs an hour, less the cost of the materials for making the bed. Evenings were spent in the veteran boxer's gym where Journée worked at teaching his lumbering charge the rudimentary skills of boxing. The going was hard. Not only had the Invincible Juan never been taught how to deliver or block a punch; his physique, largely conditioned by wrestling and weight-lifting, was all wrong for the noble art of pugilism. He had developed powerful contracting muscles but poor extending muscles, essential to a boxer's speed. Journée kept patiently at his task and at the end of three months he decided enough had been achieved to merit a letter to his former manager, Léon Sée.

In Paris, Sée read Journée's account of how he had discovered this young giant working in a fairground, how he had been teaching him to box, and how he was now convinced he could offer Sée a potential heavyweight champion of France and possibly, given a few years, of the world. He, Journée, would play his part in the training and would split his commission of 35 per cent with Sée, right down the middle. In 1928, Sée was 51 years old, with an established European reputation and an English wife who had given him six children. He was not yet ready to retire, but neither was he willing to travel the four hundred miles to Arcachon to inspect a 21-year-old circus freak who, at the most optimistic, would need an investment of years and money before he could hope to go for the big prizes. He wrote back to Journée, saying he was not interested. Undeterred, Journée kept up the pressure on Sée, who finally gave way and took the train to Arcachon. He was standing with his old friend outside the gym when Primo Carnera came trudging down the road towards them.

'[He was] clothed in veritable rags, trousers that came only halfway down his legs, enormous feet in rope sandals so small that his toes poked out like those of a clown, and with an 8-day growth of beard. He walked heavily, head sunk in shoulders, his feet dragging in the dust.'*

Journée begged his old manager to take a look at Carnera stripped off and moving around the ring. The three months of rigorous training had already begun to pay off. Anatomically, the Italian was now shaping up more like a pugilist than a fairground strong man, and his shadow-boxing and footwork were not unimpressive for one of his size. But Sée remained undecided until Carnera stepped out of the ring and approached him, his great brow creased in anxiety.

'Give me a chance, M'sieur,' he pleaded, 'and I promise I won't disappoint you.'

There was a hunger in the words and in the Italian's dark brown eyes that, for once, had nothing to do with eating *à sa*

* *Le Mystère Carnera*, Léon Sée. Gallimard, Paris, 1934.

faim. It reached into the little Frenchman and he came to a decision. He had a dozen boxers in training at the time; one more wouldn't break him. Journée should put Carnera on the train to Paris in two weeks' time. He would be met by Sée's chief trainer, Maurice Eudeline, who would take him in charge at Saint-Germain-en-Laye.

Now Carnera was in training full time, from when he woke up in the morning until he flopped, exhausted, into bed. Following Sée's instructions, Eudeline put him into the ring with sparring partners who worked him hard while pulling their best punches. He supervised the Italian's early morning road-work, his skipping and bag-work. He might have him chopping wood for an hour, followed by the deep and skilful massages in which the trainer – almost two feet shorter than his trainee – was a specialist. Carnera was neither given, nor did he ask, for a respite from these disciplines. And when Léon Sée returned from a visit to London and watched how his new charge handled himself with the gloves on, he knew it was time to take the next small step towards his long-cherished Great Idea. This was to create a world heavyweight boxing champion out of a premise that had become rooted in his mind ever since his own painful début as an amateur boxer. The premise – confirmed by subsequent years involved in the fight game – was that for every heavyweight novice who went on to achieve professional status, something like sixty such novices, many of them promising, would abandon the sport after being badly hurt in competition with other heavyweights before they had learned how to defend themselves. This resulted in an appalling waste of talent, for which Léon Sée blamed the boxing authorities who handed out licences to untrained young men still in the novice class. It took at least five years to make a champion, and in Sée's opinion it was vital that the would-be champion be protected from the effect of heavy punches until he was mentally and physically capable of absorbing them. Sée had always dreamed of guiding a young heavyweight along the road to boxing's most glittering prize. There was something about Carnera, oafish and mild-tempered though he was, that sparked in the little Frenchman a belief that a future title-holder from his camp was not an impossible dream, given the right planning and direction. The Italian's prodigious measurements were not a major factor in Sée's calculations, though a reach of 81 ¼ in was not to be sniffed at. Up against a top-ranking, hard-punching heavyweight, the Italian's extra height and weight would not count for much unless combined with speed, which was unlikely ever to be Carnera's forte. The fact that he was indeed a giant among men could be used to advantage in publicity terms, but the philosopher in Sée was being moved by other truths as he kept his protégé under scrutiny and encouraged him now and again to talk from his heart. The young man who had drifted to France as a penniless hobo in search of work was determined to become somebody his mother and fellow-countrymen could be proud of. And he knew the meaning of loyalty; he could no more betray a friend than he could squeeze his great bulk into a boot box. One could sense this after spending no more than an evening in his company.

Since Sée's return to Paris, Carnera had been asking, respectfully, to be put to work professionally, so he could start to pay back the manager for his investment. So Sée made an appointment to call on Jeff Dickson, an American long domiciled in France who, as a promoter, had done more than anyone to put spectator sports such as tennis, 6-day cycling, boxing and ice hockey on the European sporting map. Dickson, like Sée, was small in stature but big in his thinking. Imperturbable and suave, he was as different from the typical sports promoter as it was possible to be, and perhaps because of this was a favourite with the press and much respected by his peers in the sporting world. Sée's intention was to talk Dickson into setting up a match for Carnera, preferably in the great Salle Wagram in Paris, where the promoter held sway, and only against an opponent conformable with the Great Idea. But knowing Dickson as he did, he would have to pull something of a stunt if he were to pique the American's interest.

On arriving for the appointment, Sée left the now custom-suited and homburg-hatted Carnera in the anteroom before

walking alone into the promoter's office. Sée's own account* of
what followed was never refuted by Dickson.

'My dear friend, I've brought you a flyweight who in my
opinion has great promise. Could you fix a fight for him on your
next programme?'

'What's his name?'

'Oh, you wouldn't have heard of him. His name is Carnera.'

'Carnera? No flyweight of that name I've ever heard of.
Anyway, as you well know, flyweights don't pull the crowd.
Bring me a heavyweight, Léon.'

'All right, but since he's here, would you take a quick look at
my flyweight?'

'If it makes you happy – bring him in.'

Carnera's appearance, filling the doorway as he bent his head
to pass through, left Dickson speechless for a moment. Then, in
a faint voice: 'What the hell is this?'

'This is my flyweight, Jeff.'

Dickson got up from his desk and circled slowly around the
stationary Italian. He stopped beside the smiling Léon Sée.

'And he can box?'

'A little. Nothing great.'

Dickson took another slow walk around Carnera. 'Jesus, he's
two heavyweights rolled into one. If he can put up a halfway
decent show in the ring, he could be a terrific attraction. Tell
you what, Léon: how about next week at the Salle, against
Leon Sebillo, for a thousand francs?'†

At that time, in France, this was far more than any boxer
could expect to earn for his first prize fight. But Leon Sebillo,
although only a passably good heavyweight, was a puncher and
could easily sabotage Sée's Great Idea by shaking Carnera's
confidence both in himself and his management. As the
Frenchman hesitated, Carnera spoke up.

'Please, M'sieur Sée, I'm not afraid of this Sebillo.'

But Sée's own fears persisted, to the extent that, just before

* Op. cit. pp. 42–4.
† The equivalent of £10 in 1928.

the fight, he offered Sebillo 500 francs to take a dive. Sebillo, who at the weigh-in had gaped at the sight of the towering Carnera's reshaped body (Sebillo weighed 72lb less) needed no heavy persuasion. He could do without taking a lethal sucker-punch from this unknown but formidably muscled titan.

Carnera's entry into the ring was greeted by a corporate gasp of awe from the paying public. The excitement mounted throughout the first round as the young giant stalked menacingly after the wary veteran. It exploded into near hysteria in the second round when Sebillo left his guard open just long enough to admit a right uppercut that laid him out for the count. It was nice acting and totally convincing as far as the spectators and his opponent in the ring were concerned. A time would come when Carnera would have to face the truth about his brilliant early career, but not yet, not while his self-confidence was being cemented by the little man with the Great Idea. And it was of no real concern to Jefferson Dickson whether the rest of the fights in 1928 were fixed, or how much was paid for the dives. He set up the bouts in cahoots with Sée; Sée took care of the politics – or, more to the point, the economics.

It has to be said that there was nothing novel about Sée's Great Idea except the fact that, in Europe, its essential precondition – a series of 'arranged' fights – was nowhere near the state of the art it had reached in the USA. The money to be made from prize-fighting on that side of the Atlantic was such that for a promising newcomer, especially in the heavyweight class, to be 'carried along' for his first dozen or more bouts was a practice acknowledged by all except the more gullible of fight fans and, for their own good reasons, some of the reporters in the ringside press seats. And hardly ever had the custom led to the eventual triumph of a 'paper tiger'. The legendary Jack Dempsey's road to the title was strewn in the early years by 'fixes' with the venal managers of his carefully chosen opponents.

The Salle Wagram was sold out for the second fight, with five hundred would-be customers locked out at 9 pm. Carnera's purse was raised to 3,000 francs of which half went, without his knowledge, to his opponent Joe Thomas. This was another useful heavyweight, who lasted until the third round, when he failed to rise from the canvas, to wild applause from the spectators, unaware they were paying tribute to a *coup de théâtre* rather than a *coup de poing*. A month later, on 30 October, it was a certain Luigi Reggirello's turn to lose, by a technical knockout this time, in the Cirque de Paris. No acting was called for in this instance. Money did change hands from Sée to Reggirello's manager, but the latter's fighter jibbed on the night about taking a dive, whereupon the manager, clearly a man of principle, fell back on another strategem for honouring his agreement with Sée. Reggirello had always favoured just a small glass of port before heading for the ring. It steadied his nerves without adversely affecting his performance. By an unusual concatenation of circumstances, all the preliminary bouts at the Cirque on 30 October were going the full length, thus leaving Luigi and his compatriot Primo kicking their heels in their dressing rooms long beyond the expected summons to the ring. Luigi's manager would undoubtedly reproach himself later for having so thoughtlessly left the full bottle of ruby port exposed in Reggirello's dressing room while he took a stroll around the arena with a friend. But to the thousands who had paid to goggle at boxing's latest phenomenon and at the glazed eyes, wobbly legs and final cave-in of Carnera's opponent in the third round, no explanation was needed but the obvious one: the terrible impact of the mammoth Italian's punches.

The truth, which seemed to elude even the veteran sports writers at the ringside that night, was that Carnera had not yet developed anything like a real knockout punch. He was immensely strong and surprisingly light on his feet for a man of his weight, but he lacked the ability to combine power with speed and precision and, most of all, he lacked the killer instinct that the 'Manassa Mauler', Jack Dempsey, had defined as 'never letting up so long as the other guy is still standing'. He had no compunction about aiming blows at an exposed chin or solar plexus, and if this resulted in his opponent being counted out or giving up the fight, all well and good. But his intention was not so much to hurt as to put his opponent *hors de combat*. This seemed an easy enough matter, even without putting all his strength into a punch. And that is how it seemed, or seemed to seem, to those French reporters who wanted their readers to share the privilege of being in at the birth of a prodigy.

Incongruously, it fell to the journalists of Carnera's own native Italy to be the first to call in question the genuineness of the reputation that was being so sedulously fostered in Paris. As the news from that city reached the sporting circles of Milan, a boxing promoter named Carpegna made an offer to Sée of 12,000 francs for Carnera to meet the 25-year-old black South American, Epifanio Islas, in Milan's Palazzo dello Sport on 25 November. Sée turned away from the bait. Islas was 6 ft 4 in. tall, weighed 225 lb and was technically more than a match for Carnera. It was a nice fat purse, but what if Islas was not interested in taking a fall? Carpegna kept at it and, to end the matter with face, Sée demanded an outrageous 25,000 francs which Carpegna, after swallowing hard, agreed to, thereby putting Sée on the hook. In the event, the Frenchman succeeded, on arrival in Milan, in making a deal with Islas, and all would have been well if the black boxer had not made such a flop – in both senses – of taking his dive in the fifth round, on receipt of a right cross from Carnera that might just possibly have laid out his aged grandmother. Upon being ordered by the irate referee to get up and fight on, on pain of being disqualified and losing his purse, Islas felt obliged to go the full ten rounds with Carnera, while permitting the frustrated and tiring Italian to build up enough points to win the verdict. This was greeted with boos from the meagre ranks of the paying customers and by excoriating comments next day by the boxing critics, one of whom predicted that within a couple of months the choice left to Primo would be between going back to the fairground or resuming his early career as a carpenter. The future world champion would recover from this setback and make the critics swallow their words. But for the over-generous Carpegna there was no such satisfaction. Faced, later, with financial ruin, he committed suicide, and when Carnera heard about this he persuaded Sée to send the promoter's family a substantial sum of money out of his own account.

It was the first time in six years that Carnera had set foot in his own country, and on arrival in Milan for the Islas fight he had telephoned the post office at his native village of Sequals with a message for his mother. She was to make the 235-mile journey to Milan where she would be her son's guest for three days at the Grand Hotel Agnelli.

Giovanna Carnera, a 5 ft 8 in. powerfully built 50-year-old, arrived at the hotel around noon on the day of the fight, went to the desk and asked in her Friulano dialect to see her son. Told by the concierge that this was out of the question since signore Carnera was sleeping and could not be disturbed, she started to weep. It had been an arduous journey by buses and trains and she could no more understand the concierge than he could, or would, understand her. Happily, a passing waiter, noting Giovanna's striking facial resemblance to the boxer, asked if she were indeed his mother. She was then promptly bowed into a salon and served refreshments while the news of her arrival was conveyed upstairs.

Primo was a teenager when he set out from his impoverished village to seek work across the border in France. Now, twenty minutes after Giovanna's arrival at the hotel, a giant of a man, elegantly suited and exposing rows of half-inch teeth in a face-splitting smile, loomed over Giovanna and uttered the one word in a double-bass voice:

'Mamma!'

Giovanna knew nothing about prize-fighting and never became reconciled to the idea of a son who was paid to hurt people or suffer hurt himself. However, she stayed on with Primo for another two days and shed copious tears when they parted. Her husband, Sante, who was working in Egypt, and was as uninformed as his wife about boxing, had been delighted to receive a letter from Léon Sée earlier that year, informing him that Primo was making great progress under the Frenchman's tuition and showing distinct promise for the future. Through the good offices of a literate workmate, Sante at once dictated a letter to his son, congratulating him on doing so well in night school, or adult education, or wherever he was being taught, thus making up for the wartime deficiencies in schooling. It took a long letter from Primo, enclosing a batch of press cuttings about his first three Paris fights, to put his father in the picture. From then on, Sante followed his son's pugilistic career closely and proudly.

3
A 'Monster' Unleashed

Léon Sée had arranged with Dickson to stage one more bout for Carnera in Paris on 1 December, against a compliant heavyweight from Marseilles, Constant Barrick. To please Paul Journée, this was to be followed on 8 December by an exhibition bout between him and Primo in the south-west city of Bordeaux, thirty miles from Arcachon, where the young giant who had been causing such excitement in Paris was discovered earlier that year. Organized fisticuffs not being a particularly appropriate form of entertainment during the season of peace and goodwill to all men, there would then be a hiatus until the New Year, when Carnera and an ex-champion of Germany, Ernst Rosemann, would each be invited to batter his opponent insensible before a paying audience in Berlin. And this, in theory at least, could indeed be an outcome of the match since Rosemann, like Reggirello, was refusing all inducements to do the sensible and lucrative thing by measuring his length on the canvas to a count of ten. Faced with this threat to his Great Idea, but not yet ready to let Carnera into the secret of his early successes, Léon Sée devoted the time up until the fight in strengthening, as best he and Eudeline could, his fighter's defence and power-punching. In both respects, Carnera had in fact been showing marginal improvement since the fiasco in Milan, and on the night of 18 January 1929 he scored his first genuine victory when the referee spared Rosemann further punishment by stopping the fight in the fifth round.

The much relieved Sée now decided – rather too soon as it turned out – that he could further test his boy's progress, and at the same time economize on dive-money, by arranging a few more genuine bouts, provided the opponents were chosen with a proper regard for Primo's welfare. The German heavyweight Franz Diener seemed to fit the bill. He was having eye trouble and was ready to hang up his gloves as soon as he had raised the purchase price, by honest combat, of a butcher's shop he had his one good eye on. Perhaps it was fitting that in the Leipzig stadium on the night of 18 April 1929 he should pole-axe Carnera in the first round with a viciously illegal left hook to the Italian's groin. It would be charitable to excuse this impropriety on the grounds that Carnera, obedient as ever to Sée's instructions, had from the start been pumping his absurdly long left into Diener's eyes, thus adversely affecting their focus. But Diener's was a genuinely crippling blow and Carnera had be be helped, in great pain, to his corner. The referee's attention must have wandered at the crucial moment, for he pronounced no wrongdoing but granted the stricken Italian a five-minute respite before resuming the fight. Primo spent the five minutes groaning and vomiting. No way could he even stand up. The referee offered him a further five minutes, but despite the intervention of the president of the German Boxing Federation with the command, 'You haf to continue ze fight!' Carnera remained *hors de combat*, whereupon he was disqualified and his purse sequestered.

This should have taught Sée the folly of such bromides as 'Let the best man win' and put him back on the track of his Great Idea. But Dickson had set up three successive 'clean' dates in Paris with opponents who, he assured his colleague, were capable of giving Carnera a fair fight without serious risk to his person or a drain on Sée's contingency funds. In the event, the Paris spectators were given a better than ever show for their money with a points win for Carnera over ten rounds against Moise Bouquillon and technical knockouts of Marcel Nilles and Jack Humbeeck, in rounds three and six respectively.

As Primo's name increased in type size on the boulevard *affiches*, the clamour for seats grew with each new Dickson promotion, and in August 1929 the demands of a wider French public to see the 'Macaroni Colossus' in action put Sée's circus on the road to San Sebastian for a points victory over José Lete (a genuine bout) and three successive KOs, each within four rounds, in Marseilles, Dieppe and again in Paris. The last three bouts were fixed, and we have Sée's word for it. Reference has already been made to this extraordinary book, *Le Mystère Carnera*, in which the author, two years after ending his professional relationship with the fighter, sets out the record of his stewardship, including a detailed account of the professional bouts up to his parting with Carnera, with the annotation *Fixé* or *Sincère* (i.e. genuine) against each opponent on the list. Sée's motive in publishing this confession is something we will examine later. In the meanwhile, it is a reflection on the expertise – perhaps even the integrity – of European sports writers of that era that none of them, not even such ace reporters as Trevor Wignall of the *Daily Express* and Peter Wilson of the *Sunday Pictorial*, showed any sign of being aware that they and the public were being taken for a ride. The most remarkable instance of this was to come when Carnera, having made short shrift of a mediocre British heavyweight, Jack Stanley, in London's Albert Hall, was matched with a truly formidable American adversary: 'Young' Stribling.

The British had taken warmly to Primo Carnera from the day he set his 15-inch boot in London. In that October of 1929, on the threshold of the Great Depression, more photos and column inches were devoted to the Italian giant, in the popular press certainly, than to a vain Prime Minister Ramsay MacDonald or to King George V. He was mobbed whenever he appeared on the street; and in the red-light quarter of Soho, with its concentration of Italian restaurants, dark-eyed waitresses literally tore at each other for the thrill of serving his table. But more of that anon . . . Immediately after the one-round KO of Stanley, Léon Sée accepted an offer of £1,500 for Primo to appear nightly on the stage of the Alhambra Theatre of Varieties for two weeks in an unstrenuous demonstration of exercises and warm-ups with a succession of cauliflower-eared pugs, ending with a comedy routine in which the Italian protected his kneecaps from the assault of a diminutive boxer. The show was a sell-out and would have been extended but for the star's commitment to an exhibition of one-minute rounds against four amateur heavyweights up in Glasgow, where hundreds of women of all ages formed the main body of the crowd that greeted him at Queen Street station.

The Albert Hall promotion had been Jeff Dickson's first in London and his appetite was now whetted for further exploitation of the British public's interest in Carnera. He spoke with Stribling's father-manager, known to everyone as 'Pa'. Pa Stribling then hurried to London and offered on Dickson's behalf a guarantee of £2,000 against 30 per cent of the gate for Carnera to meet Young Stribling in the Albert Hall on 18 November. Léon Sée sent him smartly back to Paris with an emphatic 'Non!'. His son was then rated fourth among American heavyweights in contention for the world championship. The handsome 24-year-old 'Georgia Peach' had already won the light-heavyweight championship of the world. With over two hundred contests behind him, he was regarded as one of the most skilful boxers of that period.

A few days later, Pa Stribling is back in London with an offer Sée can surely not refuse. Young Stribling will go easy on the big Italian. He will even allow him to go the distance. It will be no disgrace, at this stage in Primo's career, to lose on points to such an opponent. Sée still refused to play. Even if he could trust the Striblings, on the night, to abide by the pact, the only effect of such a mismatch would be to expose Primo's still considerable deficiencies as a fighter. And anyway, who needed a defeat, even against such a formidable opponent? Now, if Pa Stribling would agree to a *return* match, with his boy taking a dive in one of the early rounds . . .

This was out of the question, of course. But they were reasonable men, these two managers, with a common respect for the rewards of commercial compromise. Before Pa Stribling returned to Paris the issue had been resolved through a formula worked out by Léon Sée. It was as ingenious as Gallic venality and logic could make it. There would be two bouts, the first in London, the second in Paris, both under Dickson's promotion. Around about the fourth round of the Albert Hall bout, Young Stribling would deliver a blatantly low punch that would leave Carnera writhing helplessly on the floor of the ring, unable to resume the fight. A win for the Italian on a foul; no real dent in the American's reputation. The return match would be staged – obviously to a sell-out – at the Velodrome d'Hiver on 7 December, after Primo had recovered from the cruel foul and was burning for revenge. On this occasion, and in a manner yet to be worked out, Young Stribling would be fouled by Carnera, thus levelling the score, thrilling the fans and opening the way to another and even more dramatic revenge match some time in the future, with no loss of status meanwhile to either boxer.

Sée was left with just one problem: Carnera would obviously have to be a willing participant in the two charades. So far, he had obeyed Sée in everything that touched upon his career and in the process had gained a degree of self-esteem he had never before enjoyed. How would he react to being manipulated like this, and to the light it would throw upon all those easy victories of the past year and a half? There is no record of how Sée went about it, but from the fact that Carnera fell in with the plan we can assume that the Frenchman and one-time student of philosophy knew perfectly well how to soothe wounded pride with the balm of logic. And in this he would have been aided by a circumstance totally unrelated to his management duties. Primo had fallen in love. She was a 19-year-old waitress named Emilia Tersini, born in England of Italian parents and working at Molinari's in Soho, Primo's favourite restaurant in London. She was a dark-eyed five-foot-seven with curly black hair and a pale complexion that prettily set off her blushes whenever the boxer loomed through the restaurant's Frith Street entrance. He had met Emilia's parents and had told Sée about his honest intentions towards the girl. Sée had been wise enough not to interfere in the affair, which indeed was innocent enough, but had suggested that the loving couple put all thoughts of matrimony aside until his fighter could support them both in a manner to which neither had been accustomed, but nevertheless deserved. And there can be little doubt that this glowing prospect was used effectively to win Primo's acceptance of the Stribling scenario.

Both fighters were now working out in London, and since there was too much at stake to risk giving the game away with unconvincing performances on the nights, the two managers set up an exercise that for sheer cynicism merits inclusion in any anthology of duplicity. Every day, after their public training sessions, the two fighters would make their way separately to an hotel off Piccadilly Circus and meet in a third-floor suite where Léon Sée and Pa Stribling awaited them, stop-watches in hand. And there, stripped and gloved, the 263 lb Italian and the 189 lb American rehearsed the critical moves that, in the event, would totally deceive not only the paying public but, as we shall see, the ringside press.

The first bout, at the Albert Hall, went more or less according to plan except for an incident in the third round when Stribling, who had perhaps become bored with holding his Sunday punches, released a perfect left hook to Carnera's jaw, putting the giant down for a count of eight. Until then, Primo had been enjoying himself vastly, chuckling aloud as his opponent repeatedly clinched to avoid his probing left reach. The unexpectedness and force of the hook wiped the smile from Primo's face and he came up with his huge teeth bared in a ferocious snarl, leapt at Stribling and sent him sprawling for a count of nine with one sweep of his right hand. In the corner, at the end of the round, Sée appeared to be calming his fighter and perhaps persuading him that the inadvertent left hook was hurting honest Young Stribling more than it hurt Primo. At all events, the fourth round opened with more clinches as Stribling strove to position himself to deliver the pre-ordained foul, which was perpetrated halfway through the round with an impressively wicked right, delivered well below the belt with all the force of a dessert spoon dipping into a rice pudding. And here let us quote two separate expert observers seated in the press section that night:

> Trevor Wignall, *Daily Express*: '. . . Carnera let out a howl that must have been heard in the back rows of the Albert Hall, slithered down and rolled from one side of the ring to the other.'

> John Macadam, the *Star*: 'The moment of truth[!] came in the middle of that unforgettable fourth round . . . Stribling drove a hard blow, very low, to the body. And with a sigh like a punctured balloon, Carnera sank to the canvas. Then, in an agony that was pitiful to behold, he rolled over and over to the roar of a crowd oblivious to the fact that Stribling had been sent to his corner and disqualified.'*

Among the ringside spectators was the 35-year-old Prince of Wales, later King Edward VIII and the Duke of Windsor, whose vexed royal expression boded ill for the dastardly American should he ever come calling at Windsor Castle. But if Primo Carnera made his début as a dramatic actor that night, he deserved an Oscar for his performance at the Velodrome d'Hiver three weeks later. By now, the popular press on both sides of the Channel, only too prone to exaggerate his gigantism, had stimulated such an interest and curiosity among women that, as some accounts had it, there were more females present than males at the Velodrome, including an authentic living legend, the film star Pola Negri. Special planes and trains were laid on to transport the fans from London to Paris and it was reported that 30 per cent of the passengers were women. They had come to watch the giant Italian show that he could lay the American out without fouling, and they were in for a spectacular, if unexpected, performance. For his part, Léon Sée was concerned only that the Striblings would not renege on the

---

* Again, in a recollection published on 7 July 1958, Macadam described this first Carnera *v.* Stribling bout as if it had been absolutely straight.

agreement whereby at the end of the sixth round – not before or later – Carnera would be disqualified for raining punches on his opponent after the bell had sounded.

Sée's instructions to his fighter had been precise: for the first five rounds he was to concentrate on scoring whatever points Stribling left himself open to, while keeping up an effective defence against whatever the American threw at him. Halfway through the sixth round he was to start to go on the attack. Stribling would respond by swapping punches and the two of them would get the crowd all fired up by slugging it out to their hearts' content, without going for a kill, of course. There would appear to be very little advantage, one way or the other, until twenty seconds before the end of the round, when Sée would yell out loudly, 'Go, Primo!' That would be when Carnera would appear to go for broke, throwing lefts and rights from all angles, which Stribling would easily enough block or duck while on the retreat. When the bell sounded for the end of the round, Carnera would totally ignore it and continue to rain blows on his defenceless opponent, who would have dropped his guard as he returned to his corner. The assault would be kept up for several seconds, despite the referee's attempt to stop it.

There was just one flaw in the scenario, as Professor Ivan Pavlov would undoubtedly have pointed out had he been in on the scheme. And, given Carnera's essential decency and disciplined nature, it was all too predictable a snarl-up. Over the first five rounds, Young Stribling gave a credible impression of respecting his huge opponent too much to abandon caution and go in slugging. But halfway through round six, to the roars of the crowd, he stepped up the action and Carnera responded in kind, happily. Soon, stop-watch in hand, Sée yelled, 'Go, Primo!' but his voice was drowned by the clamour from the ringside spectators, all yelling their own advice to one or other of the boxers. When the bell sounded, the Italian immediately lowered his gloves and ambled dutifully back to his corner. Stribling, after a moment's puzzled hesitation, gave a shrug and followed suit.

Léon Sée was aghast. Pa Stribling stared at him from across

the ring with a slit-eyed look that said, all too plainly, 'What kind of frog trick do you think you're pulling, bud?' Carnera, coping with more or less the same query from his manager, could only mumble, 'I'm sorry, M'sieur Sée, there was so much shouting and – I just forgot.'

Sée made covert signals to Pa Stribling, indicating that everything would be put right in the next round. And, having pleaded with Sée to shout louder next time, Carnera put on the aforementioned Oscar performance.

Mention has been made about the way the experts of the press of that period were taken in by these capers. 'Today,' wrote Wignall after the Paris fight, 'there are rumours that the fight was a fake . . . No one in his senses who saw the contest will agree with these absurd yarns.'* A note of foreboding was struck by Hugh Cecil Lowther, the 5th Earl of Lonsdale, founder of the Lonsdale Belt for boxing and president that year of the recently reconstructed British Board of Boxing Control. Greatly disturbed by Carnera's 'ferocious' performance at the Velodrome, Lord Lonsdale declared, 'We are not acting in the best interests of boxing if we give Carnera our support.'† But for a fulsome though unconscious tribute to Carnera's thespian talent, one can hardly do better than quote from an account published as recently as 1984 by the distinguished Italian journalist and author, Aldo Santini. He sets the scene by describing how Stribling, quickly exploiting a gap in Carnera's defence, delivers an 'explosive' uppercut to the chin.

'The surprise and humiliation caused by the blow released what was usually one of the most carefully hidden of Carnera's emotions: his wounded pride. And the Paris public were treated to an unforgettable spectacle. The Friulano's features were transformed into monstrous savagery. The polite and generally gentle and bashful person became in an instant a primitive being, out of the stone age and primeval

* *Daily Express*, 9 December 1929.
† *News Chronicle*, 16 December 1929.

forest. He let out a scream, then a roar and then an animal howl and leapt upon Stribling, his great arms whirling. Carnera was no longer a boxer but a beast with gloves on. Incredibly tall, terribly menacing, his great chest swollen with rage, he loomed over Stribling and delivered a hurricane of punches. With the crowd on its feet, Stribling backed into his corner, trying desperately to protect himself. The bell sounded but Carnera continued to slug Stribling, who slid to the ground, groaning. Léon Sée, the referee, Pa Stribling, all the seconds grappled with Carnera and he sent them all sprawling in a heap. This was Gulliver with the face of Frankenstein.'*

The truth – unless Léon Sée was an incorrigible liar – was that this, in fact, was 'Professor Frankenstein' Sée's creation turning in a superb performance as a monster. In his own account of that last round, Sée wrote:

The seventh round was an exact repetition of the sixth, but this time everything went according to plan. To atone no doubt for his error, Carnera surpassed himself. On hearing my shout, he leapt at his opponent, just as he had in London, and was transformed in a flash into a bloodthirsty wild beast, a man-killer, continuing his frenzied assault well after the bell had sounded. It was an indescribable scene. As Stribling collapsed, each of us then improvised the roles we had to play. Pa Stribling leapt into the ring to protect his 'swooning' son. The referee tried to intervene but Primo backhanded him to the ropes. I and my helpers tried to subdue the Italian, grabbing his arms and wrists. He shook us off like a wild boar under attack by a pack of dogs. As I grabbed him again by the arm, he muttered to me, against the bedlam from the crowd, 'Is this all right?'. 'Great,' I muttered back. 'Carry on.' Finally, when the referee declared Stribling the winner by a foul, the crowd erupted in loud and prolonged protest.†

* Santini, op. cit., p. 43. Passage freely translated from the Italian.
† Santini, ibid., p. 95, et seq.

Léon Sée died in 1963 without ever retracting what he had written about Carnera and the conspiracy with the Striblings, or ever being called upon to do so. His account was published in France in 1934. It was pointedly ignored by the sports reporters who had attended the two fights and when the Paris correspondent of the *Sunday Dispatch*★ invited Pa Stribling to confirm or deny Sée's story, he said he was 'not interested in commenting'. The same curious detachment was shown by Carnera's new management, speaking for the fighter. What they must have said to restrain their lawyers from leaping into action is not on record.

The Stribling bouts were staged for no other purpose than to make money. We can only guess at what would have happened had the two fighters been allowed to confront each other with simple violence in mind, though educated opinion at the time would most probably have given Young Stribling at least a points win and possibly even a technical knockout inside the distance. But it has to remain conjectural, given the genuine progress Carnera had already made in ringcraft and punching-power by the time he made his début in London. And it is not irrelevant that whereas Young Stribling would twice lose to Jack Sharkey over the next three years, Primo Carnera, in a genuine contest, would take the heavyweight championship of the world from the same Sharkey in less than four years.

Interest was now being aroused among promoters in the United States, where the two Stribling bouts had been fully reported. But before setting out for the Mecca of prize-fighting and the rewards thereof, there was the unfinished business of Franz Diener and the robbery of the Leipzig purse to be attended to. Herr Diener being still short of the purchase price for his coveted butcher's shop, Jeff Dickson was able to persuade him to make the trip to London for a return bout with Carnera, no strings attached. This time, with no Leipzig referee in his corner, Diener was efficiently punched to a standstill over six

★ 5 August 1934.

rounds that greatly impressed one particular person at the ringside. This, once again, was the 35-year-old heir to the imperial throne of Great Britain, the Prince of Wales, destined to become King Edward VIII six years later and then the Duke of Windsor upon throwing in the towel after another kind of title fight with the Archbishop of Canterbury.

The evening was at least as notable for the unusually large presence of the gentle sex and the fervour of their support for the young giant. Females far outnumbered males at the ringside, and in the cheaper seats they were in full cry throughout the bout. While the men, for the most part, gave Diener their vocal support, the women goaded their Italian gladiator on with yells of 'Hit him!' and 'Knock him out!' It was a revealing insight into the psyche of a certain class of female and a phenomenon that recurred throughout Carnera's prize-fighting career. As late as 1933 in that career, after the Carnera v. Uzcudun fight in Rome, Pope Pius XI publicly spoke of being shocked by the abundant presence of women 'at such exhibitions of force'.

In addition to transforming Carnera from a fairground freak into a professional boxer, Léon Sée had made it his business to add conventional polish to the big man's natural good manners and to encourage his inbred Italian fastidiousness in grooming and sartorial turnout. Carnera and his manager were invited to sup with the Prince and his friends that night, and if the royal party was expecting to play host to a dumb and socially awkward prize-fighter, there was a surprise in store. Bespoke-tailored in his Savile Row dinner jacket, black hair slicked back in brilliantine gloss, his huge hands trimly manicured and his deep bass voice modulated to suit the occasion, Carnera was a tribute to his manager's tuition and his own good instincts. The supper party took place at the house of the Prince's good friend, Lord Birkenhead, and as guest of honour the Italian was seated on the right of the Prince, in clear view of the nervous Léon Sée who was seated across the table between two bejewelled and vivacious ladies of the Prince's private circle. When it became clear that the boxer was more fluent in French than in English, the entire company immediately switched to French.

Now that he could eat every day *à sa faim*, Carnera's appetite, unappeased for so many years, was usually indulged on a gargantuan scale. A typical meal consumed at Molinari's, under the enraptured gaze of Emilia Tersini, might begin with a big helping of hors d'oeuvres and go on to a pailful of minestrone, a plateful of chicken and rice, a large steak with two vegetables, a huge helping of cherry pie and a fresh pear. A normal breakfast could consist of two portions of grapefruit, two Dover soles, a 1½ lb steak with two eggs and a large dish of peaches and cream. He had eaten only a light midday meal on the day of the second Diener fight and by the time he took his place at the supper table he was famished. The meal that followed was certainly not frugal, but it amounted, all four courses, to little more than a snack for the ravenous boxer. Nevertheless, and to his manager's relief, he paced his eating to that of the others and used the right cutlery throughout the meal. Only afterwards, as he and Sée were driven back to their hotel by the Prince's liveried chauffeur in a Rolls-Royce bearing the royal crest, did he venture a critical comment. 'Oh, yes – ' he replied in answer to Sée's, 'Wasn't that an exciting experience?' ' – except for the meal, which was all right for a bantam-weight like the one sitting on my left.'

Trevor Wignall had allowed his pen to run away with his judgement when he reported, after the return bout with Diener: 'Carnera gave the finest display of boxing skill since the great days of Georges Carpentier.' True, the butcher-designate had been knocked down ten times in an unfixed fight; but Diener was by then a pushover in both senses, and to compare his opponent with one of the all-time greats of pugilistic techniques was risible. Nevertheless, Carnera was improving in skills and self-confidence with every fight. And under Sée's unremitting disciplines he had shed every ounce of superfluous fat and was now muscled for action rather than leverage. For someone scaling more than 260lb, he could move with astonishing speed, and although he never seemed to be able to punch his weight (fortunately, perhaps) a crisp slam from either of his fists could flatten most heavyweights he would come up against. And so far, with the exception of that unrehearsed left hook from Young Stribling, he had never – *grâce à* Léon Sée – known what it was like to be really hurt in the ring. As a consequence, he was inclined to treat every fight as a fun-filled exercise, more like a training session with a sparring partner, with the difference that each new bout brought an ever-increasing flow of money, some of which at least found its way into his own pocket.

As 1930 dawned, the happy-go-lucky young giant was about to learn what the fight game was really all about.

4
New York! New York!

For a year and a half now, Léon Sée had been presiding over
Carnera's training with all the dedication of a racehorse owner
obsessed with the thought of producing a winner of the Grand
National. Driven by faith in his Great Idea, he had shepherded
his protégé through a dozen and a half European prize-fights in
as many months without once exposing him to the kind of
punishment that could undermine or destroy a novice's self-
confidence. And he had now, with the Stribling scenario,
managed the minor psychological miracle of persuading a
basically scrupulous, if naïve, young Italian that a fixed fight,
here and there, was not only acceptable among professionals but
a *sine qua non* of access to the world title. Primo would not, of
course, be ready to take his place in any short list of contenders
for at least another three years. This was the time it would take,
in Sée's objective judgement, for his fighter to graduate from a
highly promising pugilistic novelty to a serious challenger for
the sporting world's crown of crowns. And, in the meantime,
there was another indispensable condition: a working tour of the
United States, for the experience, the money and the further
embellishment of an image that was already attracting the
attention of Stateside managers.

One of these, a veteran of the game, was Walter Friedman, a
New Yorker who happened to be on a scouting tour of Europe
that winter of 1929. He had seen the two Stribling bouts, and

despite what his tutored eye had told him about them – indeed, possibly *because* of that, among other things – he lost no time in propositioning Léon Sée. As the Frenchman already knew, any foreign boxer seeking a licence to fight in the USA was legally obliged to engage a licensed American manager in addition to the manager he might already be contracted to. It meant, of course, a double drain of commission from the fighter's earnings since boxers' managers, unlike authors' or actors' agents, do not believe in splitting commissions, or any of that crypto-commie nonsense. There was another reason, apart from the law, why young Primo would need a US manager with the right connections: some rather unpleasant, even unscrupulous, people were involved in the American fight game. One did not have to wait for a future movie starring Marlon Brando to be aware of that. Walter Friedman had been in the game for many years. He was respected. More than that, he had close and powerful associates in New York who would see to it that Primo and Léon were given a fair deal.

And if by a 'fair deal' Friedman was guaranteeing a well-promoted début and a well-planned initial series of fights throughout the United States, he was as good as his word. After a quick trip to Sequals to spend Christmas with his family, Carnera, together with Sée, Eudeline and a graphic artist named L. G. Berings (of whom more later) embarked on the *Berengaria* and arrived in New York on 31 December 1930. This was no longer the paradise of a million would-be immigrants' dreams; it was the United States of Herbert Hoover, presiding over unrestrained capitalism. The Wall Street crash of October 1929 had put a decisive boot into the boom–slump economy and unemployed New Yorkers who had escaped being splattered on the sidewalks by bankers jumping from skyscraper windows were in block-long lines for soup kitchens. But the Depression had not seriously dampened the entertainment industry. Misery did not seek its mirror image for company. Instead, it looked for novelty, for spectacle, for whatever would offer relief from sombre reality – something Nero had well understood, several centuries earlier. The 'talkies' had arrived, radio entertainment was hugely popular, and if there was ever a good time for a novel attraction to be introduced into the fight game, this was it.

The New York press had been fulsomely briefed by Friedman about Carnera while the boxer was still on the high seas, and the tabloids of the city were as ready to be impressed and as prone to hyperbole as their British counterparts had been. '. . . In round numbers, Carnera is 6 ft 10 in. tall, weighs 287 lb in fighting trim . . . wears a number 21 collar, a number 18 shoe and plays chess with fire hydrants.' (Don Skeme of the *New York Herald Tribune*). His weight was such, wrote a tongue-in-cheek *Daily Mail* reporter, that the *Berengaria* officers 'sighed with relief as the Italian stepped off the ship and enabled it to return to an even keel'.

Within days of his arrival Carnera was a celebrity, mobbed whenever he appeared on the street, especially by the expatriate Italians of whom almost two million had settled in New York. Most of the early publicity gimmicks, such as a shop-window display of one of the boxer's shoes with a baby doll seated in it, were inspired by the ballyhoo specialists hired by Friedman. But there was unpaid promotion from such ace reporters as Damon Runyan, who dubbed the giant from Northern Italy the 'Ambling Alp'. And Léon Sée made his own characteristic contribution. He had correctly anticipated, back in Europe, that the emphasis would be on Carnera's physical dimensions, which was all right as far as it went but ought to be leavened with a little respect for his other less earthy qualities. Such as – ? Well, he was Italian, wasn't he? And Italy had bestowed upon the world some of the greatest of graphic artists. Carnera was not exactly in that category, but he was more than just a dumb prize-fighter. He was a talented draughtsman, with a nice line in caricature and joke drawings. Here, take a look at these samples, and you can publish them in your paper if you like. No fee required.

This was where L. G. Berings, Carnera's 'drawing master' and the only honest-to-God artist in the entourage, came in. He was a fast sketcher, and never was this gift more welcome than on the occasion when, during one of the early training sessions, a cartoonist on the staff of a New York newspaper approached Sée with a transparently mischievous request. He, himself, he confided ingratiatingly, had no doubt at all that the caricatures published the day before in a rival newspaper were the unaided work of Primo Carnera. But in some unfriendly circles it was being said that the big fella was conning the press by handing out drawings done by someone else altogether – a *real* artist. He was wondering if Primo would be willing to knock off some kind of sketch right in front of him? Nothing elaborate, you understand. Just enough to enable him to kill these malevolent stories.

Telling the cartoonist that he would see how Carnera felt about that, Sée signalled to Berings to join him in the boxer's dressing room, where they quickly agreed upon the best way to handle this threatening situation. Berings would pencil on the second page of his sketch pad a caricature of the cartoonist, draped in his distinctive check-patterned overcoat with the turned-back cuffs. On meeting the cartoonist, Carnera would propose a quick sketch of the man and would position him in profile, to conform with Berings' drawing, and pretend to be sketching on a blank page of the book. When 'finished' he would tear off the page with the real sketch on it and hand it over with his compliments. All this was put to Carnera while he was dressing after a shower. Berings' sketch pad and a pencil were put into his jacket pocket and the American was invited into the dressing room.

To Léon Sée's anguish, he promptly shed his overcoat before taking up the pose suggested by Carnera. It says something for the rapport between the manager and his boxer that the latter caught on immediately when Sée, out of the American's sight, pointed to the discarded overcoat and, with one finger, 'drew' a bold check pattern across his own jacket. Carnera quietly turned over the blank page of the pad, took a quick look – his first – at Berings' sketch, and called out to the cartoonist in his still stumbling English: 'Your coat – I like dat. Good to draw, yes. Please?' The American obligingly put his coat back on and resumed his pose. Carnera went through the motions of drawing, then tore out the second page and presented it to his sitter, with apologies for the fact that his hand might have been a little unsteady from recent exertions in the ring. 'But it's fine, Primo,' the cartoonist assured him. 'I never doubted it would be. You Italians are such excellent natural artists.'

Despite Sée's announcement on arrival in New York that Carnera was 'ready to meet any boxer, regardless of race or colour, creed or size, inside a ring or outside one, with or without a referee', and useful as all this image promotion was at the outset of the Italian's American tour, Sée was aware of how much scheming lay ahead before his fighter could come anywhere near to a challenge for the title. It helped that he was still only 22 years old and that the era of such formidable champions as Jess Willard, Jack Dempsey and Gene Tunney seemed to have come to an end with the latter's retirement in 1928 as undefeated champion of the world. But before Carnera could hope to join any short list of contenders he would have to build an impressive record, in the ring, as a crowd-pleaser and money-spinner. This would need to be established right across the United States; and all the way along there would be more pitfalls, more perils than Virgil ever dreamed up for the voyage of Aeneas from Troy to the Tiber. And it would be true even with the 'insurance' offered by Friedman's colleagues, whom Sée was about to meet. Without them, or an equally venal and resourceful bunch of operators, Carnera and his entourage might just as well take the next boat back to Europe.

Sée was introduced to Friedman's friends at Duffy's restaurant on 48th Street, between Broadway and 6th Avenue.* This was one of several speakeasies operated by 'Big Bill' Duffy in junior partnership with his friend Owney Madden during the prohibition years of 1919–33. Duffy was in fact seven years older than Madden, but he lacked the racketeering drive and mobster connections enjoyed by his partner in crime. Both men

---

* Access to the restaurant and the gym on the floor above used to be through the door numbered 158, now sandwiched between Manny's Musical Instruments and Sam Ash's Drum Shop.

were products of the era of wild lawlessness in Manhattan that preceded the institutionalizing of crime by the Mafia families. The city then was carved up among territorial gangs such as the Five Pointers, the Eastmans and the Gas Housers, operating on the Lower East Side, and the Gophers, a band of thugs terrorizing the area known as 'Hell's Kitchen', between 7th and 11th Avenues and 14th and 42nd Streets. These were not cold-eyed soft-spoken *mafiosi* under the benign rule of a Godfather: they were a rabble of brutes from the cesspits of society, living on vice, intimidation and robbery with violence, and beholden only to the shifting favours of local politicians and a largely corrupt police force.

Owney Madden was born in England and taken to New York in 1902 by his father, at the age of 11 years. At 17, he was already one of the most audacious of the Gophers and by the age of 21 he had taken control of one faction of the gang and was known to the underworld as 'Owney the Killer'. The title was well deserved. He had already committed two murders and been saved from the consequences by the sudden disappearance of eye-witnesses. By 1914, he had a total of five unpunished murders chalked against him by the police. Then his luck ran out. Arrested for the killing of a fellow-gangster, 'Little Patsy' Doyle, and convicted in 1915 of first-degree manslaughter by the State's evidence of two gangland molls, he was given a 10–20-year sentence and sent to Sing Sing. After being paroled in 1923, he stayed away from his old gang and teamed up with such 'heavies' as 'Big Frenchy' de Mange, Dutch Schultz and Jack ('Legs') Diamond, for whom he acted first as an enforcer and hit-man and then as a fully fledged partner in the illegal breweries and speakeasies that flourished during the era of Prohibition. One of the breweries under his control had a daily output of 300,000 gallons of beer, delivered every night to appointed drops in New York City and New Jersey.

By the time he became involved with Primo Carnera, Madden had interests in a whole array of night-clubs, hotels, slot machines, lottery games and other prize-fighters. Described by a contemporary writer as 'sleek, slim and dapper, with the

gentle smile of a cherub and the cunning and cruelty of a devil', [*]
he had the self-confidence to match his cunning. In 1929, with a
parole violation hanging over him, he petitioned Franklin
Delano Roosevelt, then the Governor of New York State, for
permission to apply for US citizenship. FDR turned him down.
In 1932, while back in prison and with the entire nation in
trauma over the kidnapping of aviation hero Charles Lindberg's
baby, Owney Madden declared that if he were set free he would
find the baby. Lindberg finally stopped pressuring the State
Parole Board only when it turned out that Madden had
absolutely nothing to offer.

William ('Big Bill') Duffy's début in crime preceded that of
Madden's with his arrest in 1901, at the age of 17, for burglary
and his subsequent confinement in Elmira Reformatory. Seven
years later he was sentenced to 10 years in Sing Sing for armed
robbery and it was probably there that he first made the
acquaintance of Owney Madden when their terms coincided for
a while in 1914. But Duffy, born and raised in Brooklyn's tough
waterfront district of Gowanus, had by now learned how to
manipulate people. His charm – as potent a weapon, when
needed, as his aggressiveness – had already won him the favour
of the Warden of Sing Sing, one Thomas Mott Osborne, who
put him in charge of the prison's mutual welfare organization.
Whatever the post might have entailed, it turned out to be a nice
career move for Duffy, for when Osborne became head of the
US Naval Prison at Portsmouth, New Hampshire, he took good
ole Bill with him as his assistant in charge of administration.
(Yes, only in America . . .) This, in turn, opened the way for
Duffy's enlistment in the Navy and, later, to honourable
discharge as a Chief Petty Officer. And all this short of the full
term of his original sentence.

He returned to Manhattan in fine time to climb on to the
beer-wagon of Prohibition as an associate of Owney Madden,
with whom he was now able to share in a more profitable form of

---

[*] *The Gangs of New York*, Herbert Asbury (A. A. Knopf Inc., New
    York, 1928).

mutual welfare than either of them had enjoyed in Sing Sing. As a front man for Madden and Dutch Schultz, he opened a speakeasy named Club de la Vie at Broadway and 48th Street. It did great business until a gangster named Frankie Wallace had his *joie de vivre* terminated there, one evening in 1922, by an assassin no one could recall ever seeing in the joint, leave alone managing it. With understandable reluctance, the police were obliged to close the place down, but their spirits and pay-offs were restored with the opening of such Duffy-fronted establishments as the Silver Slipper and the Rendezvous. These were precisely the kind of places where fight promoters and managers liked to relax and swap matchmaking talk over bootleg hooch, and it took no time for Duffy and Madden to catch on to the moneymaking potential in the noble practice of self-defence, provided you weren't the guy actually practising it.

But Duffy, the honourably discharged Chief Petty Officer and the Warden's choice to manage the Sing Sing prisoners' welfare organization, was finding it hard to shake old civilian habits. Early in 1926, he was held in police custody for several days under suspicion of murdering a Brooklyn cabaret singer named Elsie Regan, whose body had been found in a snowbank on East 54th Street, near the East River. Duffy was picked up a few hours later, suffering from a bullet wound, but once again he had to be released for lack of evidence. And in August of that year he narrowly escaped with his life by throwing down his gun and surrendering after being chased on foot by police who wanted to talk to him about a jewel robbery.

It was about this time, in the mid-1920s, that Duffy and Madden began to exert a baleful and often brazen influence on the fight game. Writing in the *Daily Express* of 22 April 1930, Trevor Wignall recalled the fight between Jack Dempsey, who had lost his heavyweight title to Gene Tunney, and Jack Sharkey, a major contender.

Bill Duffy . . . is the owner of a somewhat celebrated night-club, and for years had been an intimate friend of Jack Dempsey. During this fight, Sharkey suddenly collapsed and claimed that Dempsey had struck him low. The referee hesitated while Sharkey grovelled on the canvas, but when everyone was wondering what was about to happen, a very loud and barked-out command was heard from someone at the ringside. The shouter was Duffy. 'Count that man!' he cried, pointing to Sharkey. The referee obeyed, and a few seconds later Sharkey lost his chance of meeting Gene Tunney for the heavyweight title at Chicago in September of the same year.

If electronic bugs and magnetic tape had been invented in 1930, there might possibly still be in existence the evidence that, at the meeting in Duffy's Restaurant, Léon Sée was offered the sum of £30,000 in return for handing over the financial control of Primo Carnera in the United States to a syndicate composed of Madden, Duffy and Walter Friedman, plus 'Big Frenchy' de Mange and Frank Churchill – two gangsters with prize-fight interests. At this time, £30,000 would have been the rough equivalent of winning a record first dividend in the football pools. Nevertheless, the Sée–Journée share of the boxer's future earnings in the USA would have been more realistically evaluated, even in 1930, at somewhere around £200,000. With the offer came an acceptance that Léon Sée would continue as the boxer's manager in Europe and that Jeff Dickson would still own 10 per cent of Carnera's earnings on the Continent, where he would also continue to enjoy exclusive promotion rights. There would be no objection to Sée's staying on in the USA with Carnera; on the contrary, it was well appreciated that for him to abandon his boxer at this crucial stage in his career could have a disastrous effect on the young Italian's morale. Sée turned down the syndicate's offer at the time. A few months later, when it came out that he had finally accepted it, the supposition was that some additional incentive, apart from money, was offered the Frenchman by these gangsters, such as insurance against accidents detrimental to his health.

Meanwhile, as far as the politics of steering the fighter towards the world title were concerned – and this remained

Sée's obsession – he need have no doubts about the practical application of his Great Idea. He was now with maestros in the art of the 'fix'. Bill Duffy would take care of Primo's programme, all the way to the contender status that was the sole basis of the syndicate's interest. Duffy would be fronting for the syndicate but would take into account Sée's opinion as to the selection of opponents and the manner of their prescribed defeats.

There remained the need of a strategy for overcoming the American authorities' ingrained hostility to the idea of a non-American winning pugilism's most glittering prize. There was no single authority regulating boxing for the whole of the United States: each state had its own athletic commission and only about twenty-five of them came under the aegis of the National Boxing Association. The more important states, such as New York, California, Michigan and Pennsylvania, had their own independent and self-regulating commissions, the most powerful of which, the New York State Athletic Commission, was essentially the juridical front for that Mecca of prize-fight promotions, Madison Square Garden. The Garden, a commercial corporation, was in keen and jealous rivalry with all other states for the staging of important fights and could count on its bed-fellow, the NYSAC, to make plenty of trouble for any fighters and managers who would not play ball. Duffy and Madden were aware that neither the Garden nor the NYSAC was willing to take Carnera seriously at this stage, but neither of them was indifferent to the promise of a big Italo-American gate for his début in a US ring. In the opinion of the NYSAC's wily old dictator, William Muldoon, the smart thing to do would be to put this Italian freak into the ring with any one of such ranking heavyweights as Jack Sharkey, Jim Maloney, George Godfrey, William ('Young') Stribling or Argentina's Vittorio Campolo. The New York Italians would fill the Garden's great arena; the 'Macaroni Tower' would come tumbling down and after that the other state commissions and promoters could have him.

Carnera's new management was not falling for that. It might

have suited the Striblings to pick up some easy money in
London and Paris, but there was no deal to be made with them
in New York, or with any of the other ranking contenders for the
title now left vacant by the retirement of Gene Tunney. During
the year ahead, there would have to be a series of eliminating
contests, and if Carnera was to be included in these he would not
only have to win his first fight in the USA in a spectacular
manner, but would need to carry on from there with decisive
victories in as many as possible of the great cities of the Union.
Primo Carnera was already a daily traffic-stopper on the streets
of Manhattan. Two million Italo-Americans were impatient to
see him in the ring. If the Garden wanted him under an
exclusive contract, his first New York fight would have to be
against the Canadian, 'Big Boy' Peterson. This would be a true
battle of giants, with Peterson only $1\frac{1}{4}$ in. shorter than Carnera.

The Garden management and the Commission agreed to the
match. Muldoon might have had second thoughts about it had
he known that Peterson had undertaken to accept a right
uppercut from his opponent a minute or so into the first round
at Madison Square Garden (then situated on 8th Avenue
between 49th and 50th streets). And that's how it worked out on
the night of 24 January 1930.

It was carnival. The Italians took over the Garden and
festooned it with the green, white and red flags and bunting of
their motherland. The roar that greeted Carnera as he made his
way to the ring could be heard five blocks away on Times
Square. And it erupted again as little Maurice Eudeline was
obliged, by Sée's inspired sense of theatre, to climb up on a stool
in order to help his boxer off with the gaudy silk dressing gown.
Big Boy Peterson took his dive after exactly seventy seconds of
the first round. For some of the spectators this was hardly value
for money, but for the Italians the occasion compensated in
glory for what it lacked in gore. Primo Carnera, the fighter who
had been booed in Milan, was that night created a hero to
Italian-Americans throughout the USA. And William Duffy at
the ringside, and Owney Madden listening-in at Sing Sing, saw
that it was good.

And to Primo Carnera, with his fellow-countrymen's *viva!*s *bravo!*s and cries of 'da Preem!' showering him with vocal honeydew as he made his way to the dressing room, this was more than good: it was the fulfilment of everything he had dared to wish for since the night – could it have been only sixteen months before – when the referee in the Salle Wagram declared him the winner of his first professional fight. True, the glory of that night had subsequently been dimmed by Léon Sée's sensitive but none the less sobering disclosure of his Great Idea and the premise upon which it was based. But before that there had been half a dozen fights that were genuine, and it was something, surely, for a novice like him to have achieved three points decisions and three knockouts, even against second-rate professionals.

If, in New York that night, the 22-year-old Carnera had needed to rationalize his own complicity in the Great Idea, it might have gone something like this:

'I was an ignorant, unschooled, penniless and hungry Italian hobo when Paul Journée, and then Léon Sée, took me on. And that's what I'd still be now if I had kidded myself I knew better than they how to box my way towards heavyweight contender status. As it is, I am already a celebrity in Europe and on the threshold of becoming one across the United States of America. I have already forgotten the gut-wrenching misery of constant and unappeased hunger. My suits, shirts and shoes are specially made to fit me. Wherever my work takes me, I stay in hotels, with my own private bedroom and bathroom. I have been making a lot of money, M'sieur Sée tells me, and will be making a great deal more now that I've won my first fight here in New York so decisively. It could be that "Big Boy" Peterson was paid to let that punch of mine through and stay down for the count. M'sieur Sée said nothing about this, and I didn't ask. It's better that way. As he says, if I knew in advance when and how the fellow I'm fighting is going to dive, I'd probably give the game away by my behaviour when it came to the crunch. Now, when I go into the ring and the bell sounds for "Seconds out!" and I'm alone, looking across to the opposite corner at a brawny half-naked hulk of a man trained for the sole purpose of battering other men senseless, what matters is that I should do it to him – or appear to do it to him – before he does it to me; that and the knowledge that wherever I go I carry with me the hopes of my family and my countrymen that I shall be the first and only Italian ever to win the world heavyweight title.'

But, about those brawny half-naked hulks . . . would it have occurred to Carnera that the very sight of the Italian colossus, stripped for the weigh-in before a fight, would be cause enough for an opponent to take fright and wonder what the hell he was letting himself in for? Probably not. The consensus of all who ever wrote about him, and of those who actually knew him and are still alive, is that there never was a more gentle and unassuming giant. If he ever scowled, growled or bared his teeth other than in a smile, it was part of the act he was expected to put on to spark a thrill of vicarious fear among the ringside customers. His true persona was unassuming, outgoing and almost over-eager to please. He laughed a great deal, often under the slightest, even silliest stimulation. Gushing admirers embarrassed him acutely. And there wasn't a scrap of 'killer' aggressiveness in his makeup. After his second fight with Franz Diener, which he knew he had to win, he slept fitfully, got up early and, skipping his favourite meal of breakfast, hurried around to the German's hotel to ask how he was and to apologize for the rough time he had given him in the ring.

Léon Sée, aware of the danger in it, had never tried to get the young giant to punch his full weight. The less squeamish Bill Duffy tried but failed to turn the amiable Italian into a Dempsey-style bone-crusher, though he improved the accuracy of his punching. One of the consequences of this, as we shall see, was a tragedy that almost caused Carnera to hang up his gloves for good.

Carnera would be 85 were he still alive at the time of this book's publication. Fortunately for the present writer, there exist relatives of his, daughters of Léon Sée, several former acquaintances and some top-rank journalists who, in interviews, were able to speak about Primo as they knew and remembered

him. As if in one voice, they spoke of his good and trusting
nature and quintessential decency.

5

On the Road to the Title

According to Léon Sée, all the next fights in the United States, from January to April 1930, except for the bout with Roy 'Ace' Clark, were fixed. They were staged across the continent, from Newark, New Jersey to New Orleans, from Philadelphia to Los Angeles, and eight other cities in between. Whenever possible, Carnera was matched against fighters big in physique if not in professional pride. In most cases the bouts went according to plan, with knockout victories in the first or second rounds. Between 6 February and 2 April, Carnera 'won' all twelve fights by knockouts. It was a dizzying, barnstorming tour, leaving the young Italian with only blurred images of faces and places. More than any other sport, boxing puts two contestants into such intense and unremitting eye-to-eye bonding as to engrave for ever, into each one's memory, the facial features of the other. This is the rule. The exception, amusingly provided by Carnera on one occasion, is not so remarkable, given the swift succession of opponents he had to face. Four months after 'Big Boy' Jim Sigman, the fifth of Carnera's 1930 opponents, had been counted out within a couple of minutes of the first round, the paths of the two fighters happened to cross on a street in Philadelphia. To Sigman's, 'Hi, Primo – remember me?' the young Italian could only stammer, 'Well, I – er – well, I – '

'I'm Sigman, man. Jim Sigman.'

The glimmer of recognition in Primo's dark eyes led to the

contrite and intendedly tactful, 'Hey, sorry, Jeem. We were, you know, so leetle time together, yes?'

These fleeting and totally unrehearsed encounters led to the occasional mishap on the night itself. In Chicago, the Canadian heavyweight, Elzar Rioux, was so terrified on finding himself alone in the ring with the colossal Italian that he took a dive in the opening round from a punch that could have been mistaken for a caress. When Carnera, noting the referee's scowl, yelled at Rioux to get up and fight, the Canadian did so, only to take a full count on receipt of the next punch, a right cross to the head. He was fined $1,000 by the Chicago Boxing Commission for non-fighting, and Carnera insisted on reimbursing him.

Wherever the bandwagon stopped, the best local heavyweights were hired to work as sparring partners with Carnera. This not only brought in admission money from a public eager to see the Ambling Alp in the flesh; it allowed Carnera to adapt himself to different styles of boxing. It is hard to believe Sée's assertion that he never actually told Carnera, during this all-important first tour of the USA, about the 'arrangements' with his opponents. Perhaps it was a case of Sée's wink being as good as a nod to Primo, who would have been content to leave such matters to his managers, with total confidence in their judgement. But it was Sée's lament, later, that the only matches plagued with problems were the honest ones.

This was certainly true of the bout on 3 March in Philadelphia with Roy 'Ace' Clark. Along with his height of 6 ft 8 in., the black fighter had an abnormally long reach, which he used to good effect right up to the start of the fifth round, when he unleashed a lulu of a hard right to Carnera's left eye. Almost immediately, a huge 'mouse', or swelling, as big and colourful as an orange, erupted below the eye, closing it completely. The Italian fought on as best he could and at the end of the round he refused to let Sée throw in the towel. However, the official doctor of the boxing commission took one look at the monstrous swelling and declared it too dangerously full of blood for the fight to continue. Out of long experience, Sée tried to persuade the doctor that the 'mouse' consisted not of blood but of air, a much less dangerous condition that can occur when a boxer inhales powerfully through the nose at the precise moment when a blow is delivered to the eye. For the fight to end now on a technical knockout would mean breaking the triumphant sequence of seven wins chalked up so far on the tour. Sée backed Carnera in his plea to be allowed to go on fighting and the doctor grudgingly consented to 'just one more round, no more'.

The bell sounded and Carnera, still half-blind, went surging into action against Clark. A right uppercut found the black boxer's chin and he went down for the count, leaving it a forever open question whether he was struck by remorse for the damage he had done to a gutsy opponent or genuinely put on his back.

Whatever the truth of it, Léon Sée conclusively won his argument with the doctor, back in the dressing room after the fight. Determined to prove that the 'mouse' was full of blood, the medico carefully inserted a syringe into the swelling. It instantly, and bloodlessly, deflated like a pricked balloon.

About three months later, on his return to Philadelphia for the match with George Godfrey, Carnera's manager was presented with a bill from the same doctor for a hundred dollars for 'medical attention'.

Among the opponents who turned in performances even beyond the call of booty, mention should be made of Chuck Wiggins who, on receipt of a left hook, managed a truly elegant dive through the ropes, head first, to the amazement and admiration of Carnera. But there was a limit to the long and strong arm of the New York-based syndicate that had organized the 1930 tour, and it fell short of the Oakland ball park in California where, ominously enough, the thirteenth contest was scheduled to take place on 14 April. This was against a black San Franciscan heavyweight, Léon ('Bombo') Chevalier, who had refused all inducements by Sée and Duffy to be the fall guy. The open-air park had been well sold and there was no way the bout could be cancelled without jeopardizing the publicity capital built up so far along the road. Sée was worried, as well he should have been now that Big Bill Duffy was calling the shots.

The first five rounds gave the crowd its money's worth, with the two fighters swapping punch for punch and the outcome still anyone's guess when the bell sounded for the start of the sixth round. But all was not quite how it seemed to be . . . Next day, when the California State Athletic Commission met to consider certain charges arising out of the fight, Chevalier was pressured by his wife to tell the truth. He had been offered, and had refused, $1,000 to throw the fight. Between the early rounds one of his seconds, Bob Perry, warned him he would be bumped off if he didn't dive before round ten. But Chevalier continued to give of his best, and this despite having rosin deliberately rubbed into his eyes at the start of round six. In the course of that round, the half-blinded Chevalier put Carnera down for a count of five. The Italian sprang up, smarting with hurt pride, and started to wade fiercely into his opponent. While Chevalier was still on his feet and seemingly capable of fighting on, Perry threw in the towel, contrary to Californian regulations under which only a boxer's chief second could do so. This was when the ball park crowd erupted in protest and Perry was beaten up by a group of ringsiders. Both fighters were ordered to appear next day before the commission, which meanwhile suspended Carnera's $10,000 purse. The purse was later released under threat by Sée of legal action but the commission suspended the California licences of Carnera and his three managers, Sée, Duffy and Friedman.

This was bad enough, but now the New York State Athletic Commission, which had never before adopted decisions taken by its Californian equivalent, also ordered Carnera's suspension. Any suspicions Léon Sée might have had as to an ulterior motive behind these decisions seemed to be confirmed when they remained in force despite a subsequent statement by the California Commission to the effect that Chevalier and Carnera had in fact fought an honest fight to the best of their abilities. For its part, the NYSAC could at least draw some support for its action from the report of a committee set up earlier in the year to investigate all of Carnera's bouts from his arrival in the USA. The committee's report was published on 16 May and written by General Clinnin, chairman of the Illinois State Athletic

Commission. It stated:

> 'A review of all the facts and circumstances in connection
> with the various matches of Carnera and his opponents in the
> United States led us to but one conclusion: that P T Barnum
> was correct in his observation, "The American public likes to
> be humbugged". The committee believes that a definite
> "build up" policy to establish the Italian as one of the
> outstanding heavyweights of the world has been followed,
> but found no direct proof of "criminal conspiracy" other
> than the record of the hearing after the bout with Chevalier at
> Oakland, California.'

In fact, purse sequestering and suspensions in one form or
another were imposed on Carnera almost throughout his boxing
career in the USA. They were shortlived and they ended either
under threat of legal action by the Italian's managers or for a
much simpler – almost engaging – reason. Back in the thirties,
most state boxing commissions met twice a week and the
members were on *per diem*, which meant they were paid a fixed
fee just for showing up and voting. Thus, on a Tuesday they
might meet to order a boxer's suspension. On the Friday, if
there were no other decisions calling for a vote, they could vote
to reinstate the boxer and collect their second fee for that week.*
In the case of the Chevalier affair, Léon Sée suspected a more
sinister reason for New York's apparently slavish falling in with
California. A bout for the vacant world title between Jack
Sharkey and the German heavyweight champion, Max
Schmeling, was due to take place at Madison Square Garden in
July. The Garden's management had offered $25,000 for
Carnera to fight on the same card against an easy opponent. The
effect would be a probable doubling of the gate receipts and,
equally important, an assurance that there would be no other
bout involving the Italian – now a popular attraction – around
the same date as the Sharkey–Schmeling fight. Sée had refused
the offer, saying that his boxer was already himself in the

---

* *Madison Square Garden: 100 Years of History*, Joseph Durso (Simon
   & Schuster, New York, 1979).

contender class and could beat Sharkey and Schmeling together in the same ring. Meanwhile, and to the Garden's annoyance, several other states were showing eagerness to promote a fight between the giant Italian and the black heavyweight George Godfrey, then considered a worthy contender for the title. The prospect of either of these two men being in line for the title would hardly bring joy to the Garden. Carnera, like Schmeling, was another foreigner, dammit; and seven more years would elapse before the powers behind the game grudgingly accepted the idea of a black boxer's being given a crack at the title, leave alone holding it against all comers, as Joe Louis would, for eleven more years. The Carnera–Chevalier affair seemed to offer the prospect of putting both fighters out of the running for a while at least, and in fact it was an unfortunate setback for the Italian, although he was to fight nine more times throughout the USA over the next five months.

As the tour continued, Carnera was showing steady improvement in skills against opponents who, with only a few exceptions, either wouldn't or in some cases couldn't inflict the kind of damage that would undermine Sée's Great Idea. Meanwhile, the boxer's progress with the English language could be somewhat erratic, as a certain Los Angeles disc jockey had discovered, just before the Chevalier fight. He had been warned by Sée that Carnera's English was not yet up to the standard needed for a live interview, but the disc jockey was not to be denied his on-the-air scoop. 'Look, I'll ask him just three simple questions: How much do you weigh? How old are you? How tall are you? All he has to do is come up with the simple answers, in English.'

Sée rehearsed Carnera in the sequence of questions and the appropriate answers, passed him as word perfect and settled back in the producer's booth to enjoy the mellifluous resonance of his boy's bass articulation. The snarl-up came not from Carnera's English but from the disc jockey's lapse in changing the order of his questions, starting with:

DJ: How old are you, Primo?
Primo: Two hundred and seventy-five.

In a Los Angeles barber shop that same week, Primo had summoned a manicurist who, in the bright and expectant manner of all Angelinos, then and now, asked him, 'And what do you think about LA?'

'I knock him out in two rounds,' Primo declared.

Now, once again, Léon Sée finds occasion to lament that 'We get more often into trouble with the authorities when a fight is absolutely genuine than when it is fixed.' The location is the Philadelphia ball park and the date is 23 June. (Frank Weiner, chairman of the Pennsylvania Athletic Commission, had flouted the NBA by authorizing this bout). Carnera is feeling in good form for the match with George Godfrey. He has enjoyed a month's break from fighting after disposing of another black fighter, Sam Baker, in one round at Portland, Oregon, and, three weeks earlier, had KO-ed a fighter named K. O. Christner after four vigorously battled and possibly genuine rounds in Detroit. But Godfrey – who couldn't be bought – was in another league, and easily the most dangerous opponent Carnera had yet come up against. It was a critical match in his career. His drawing power had been jeopardized by the Chevalier affair. It would come to an end if he were defeated. In the event, the fight produced nothing but trouble for both contestants. It started before either of them entered the ring, when Francis Connolly, an inspector for the Pennsylvania Athletic Commission, stalked into the Italian's dressing room and started to throw his weight around. Carnera's bandages, he declared, were not regulation. Léon Sée insisted they were; it just took extra length to make a wrapping of the huge hands. Well, his pants are not the right colour, the official weaseled on. Sée was arguing back about this when Bill Duffy walked into the room and took over in his charming Irish way. He had already clashed with Connolly in an argument over the type of abdominal shield to be worn that night by another boxer under his management, Jackie Silver.

'I'm giving you five seconds to get lost,' he told the official.

Upon the lapse of this period of grace, he floored the fellow with a left hook, dislodging three teeth, and locked him up in a vacant dressing room.

Carnera's instructions were to use his educated left to keep
Godfrey at bay over the first four rounds, after which he ought
to be able to nail the out-of-condition black. From the start, the
fighters went at each other with a good will, the 218 lb Godfrey
weaving and bobbing as he tried to slam his way through the
Italian's defence. Carnera worked with straight lefts and right
uppercuts and by the end of the fourth round, the honours were
about even. One minute and thirteen seconds into the fifth,
Godfrey – who had just been warned for a low punch – aimed
what he no doubt intended to be a legitimate left hook to the
solar plexus. It was a beauty, with his shoulder right behind it,
but it landed well below the belt, laying Carnera out. Tommy
Reilly, the referee, stopped the fight. The doctor of the State
Athletic Commission examined Carnera and confirmed the foul.
The Italian was carried to his corner by Sée, Duffy and Friedman.

But the same doctor had one more injury to examine, after the
door to a spare dressing room had been unlocked. As a
consequence, Duffy, Sée, Carnera and Silver were barred by the
NBA from all states under its control and Godfrey's share of the
purse was reduced from £2,000 to £1,000. Bill Duffy, the real
culprit, played down the significance of the ban. There were
plenty of states independent of the NBA. And the ban would be
lifted shortly, anyway. Carnera was already too big a draw with
the fight fans to be elbowed out of the East Coast scene. Max
Schmeling, Gene Tunney and Jack Sharkey had all three of
them been at the ringside to see how Godfrey would make out
against the interloper from Italy. After the fight, Godfrey
admitted to the foul. 'Yes, I hit him low, I admit it. I'm a good
nigger and I always tell the truth. Primo fouled me in the third
and fourth round, so we are about even.'

Nine weeks were to elapse before Carnera returned to the
East Coast to meet Riccardo Bertazzolo in Atlantic City after
disposing of the black American 'Bearcat' Wright in Omaha and
the Australian George Cook in Cleveland, Ohio. Of these two
bouts only the Wright one was fixed, though the bout with Cook
might have seemed to be, for all the fight the unfortunate Aussie
put up before being KO-ed in the second round. Wright, on the

other hand, gave unexpected value for money when one of the
four pillars of the ring gave way as he fell against the ropes and
ended up sprawled among the paying customers. The big
pugilist had never lost a fight by a knockout and he resented
having to spoil this record. The collapse of the pillar seemed
especially fortunate: he could delay climbing back into the ring
until the referee had finished his count of ten. He would still
lose, but his record would remain morally intact since he could
rightly claim he was on his feet, climbing back, when the count
finished. What neither of the fighters realized was that a
Nebraska rule obliged the referee to go on counting to twenty,
by which time 'Bearcat' was back in the ring, facing his equally
perplexed opponent. Now it took five men, standing on the
apron of the ring, to keep the pillar propped up as the fight went
on, and of course they were all propelled into the ring whenever
one of the heavyweights hit the ropes. The hilarious show ended in
the fourth round when Bearcat decided what-the-hell and stayed
down for the count after accepting an uppercut from Carnera.

Meanwhile, the NBA had announced a conditional lifting of
Carnera's suspension, adding that it was prepared to lift the ban
completely if the boxer would agree to sever relations with his
managers. One can imagine the reaction of Duffy and Madden
to this stipulation. They had invested only a few thousand
dollars, at most, in launching their Italian upon the American
prize-fighting scene and now, after only seven months, they had
recovered the whole of their investment and were already
showing a substantial profit. Apart from the syndicate, no one –
certainly not Carnera – was given a sight of the figures of net
earnings that first year in the USA, but when Paul Journée filed
suit in October 1930 against Sée and Carnera for his $17\frac{1}{2}$ per
cent share of commission, of which he had not then had a penny,
he claimed that Sée had already received £80,000 up to that
date. Even assuming that a portion of that sum represented
recovery of earlier investment by Sée, we are probably looking
at a figure of well over £100,000 in total commissions divisible
between all four managers up to that point. Today, that would
be the equivalent of £1 million.

Carnera's bout with Riccardo Bertazzolo on 30 August was his twenty-first fight in the US, all of which he had won but only three of which had not been fixed in advance – four if we include the questionable bout with Christner. Bertazzolo, a proud and gutsy fighter, was refusing all proposals by his manager, one Aldo Linz, that he should take a dive in return for a percentage of the gate that would earn him $10,000 against Carnera's purse of $6,000. When Linz failed to persuade him to accept even a points win by Carnera, Linz pulled a ruse out of his sordid bag of tricks that, had Carnera known about it, would surely have revolted him, hardened though he must have been by now to the iniquities of the fight game. Between the second and third rounds of the fight at Atlantic City, Linz used a concealed razor blade to make a cut just above Bertazzolo's left eyebrow, pasting over the slit immediately with vaseline. With the first blow that landed on his fighter's brow, the cut opened up, the blood flowed and the referee stopped the fight, awarding Carnera a technical knockout.*

Three final encounters were fixed for that year before Primo and company ended the American tour and headed back to Europe. These were against Pat McCarthy in Newark, New Jersey, on 8 September, Jack Gross in Chicago on 18 September and Jim Maloney in Boston on 7 October. The outcome of the first two bouts was predictable for the simple enough reason that both fighters had been told precisely when to take their dives: McCarthy in round two and Gross in round four. Maloney was a different cup of Boston tea. He couldn't be bought; he was fighting in his native city, and in the course of a professional career that had started in 1924 he had been matched against some top-ranking opponents, beating some, losing to some. Though he was now past his prime, he would put to a useful test Carnera's real potential as a future contender. This had been Sée's reason for agreeing to the bout, against the shrewder

* Linz's own testimony, several years later, as quoted by Aldo Santini. *Carnera*, Milan 1984, p. 53.

advice of Bill Duffy, who took the view that there was no way
Jim Maloney could be beaten in Boston so long as the decision
rested on the referee alone, as would be the case on this occasion.

The fight was over ten rounds. It went the distance and
Maloney was declared the winner. Impartial witnesses agreed
that Carnera had won every single round on points. This was
completely confirmed by a film of the fight, subsequently
shown in Britain, France and Italy, in the course of which the
referee is seen actually to block Carnera's right arm when it was
about to deliver what could have been a decisive uppercut. Léon
Sée's fury on being 'robbed', and his decision never again to
accept the sole judgement of a referee, might have won him
more sympathy had his own stance on pugilistic ethics been less
peccable. As it was, the one and only defeat of Carnera's 1930
tour was generally discounted by the fans and the sports writers
and it was as a hero to his own people and a continuing
fascination to others that he sailed for Europe aboard the luxury
Italian liner, the *Conte Grande*.

Hardly less a giant, physically, and certainly mentally – Paul
Gallico – had written in the New York *Daily News*: 'He steps
practically unchanged out of the limbo of things that used to
excite or frighten us. Had he but one eye in the center of his
forehead, he might pass for Cyclops. Indeed, as he climbed into
the ring in Madison Square Garden he might have stepped from
some nursery frieze or from between the covers of an
imaginatively illustrated copy of Jack the Giant Killer . . . It is
from this tribe that Carnera springs.'

Gallico's words were quoted in New York's *Literary Digest* of
1 May 1930, in the course of a full-length article about Carnera.
In similar vein, another highbrow publication, the *Literary
Review*, quoted William Bolitho's piece, published in *The
World*: 'The coming of Carnera is a major event to I do not care
to guess how many millions of men of all nationalities today. At
Detroit, or behind the Chicago stockyards, in the ruined colliery
villages of the North of England, on the quayside of Venice,
New York, and for all I know, Shanghai, they are discussing it
over their lunchpails at this very moment . . . The heavyweight

contender . . . must be the embodiment of the strange and unusual yet elemental qualities, so that grown men of imagination may adopt him and play with him. He must be material for folklore . . . a gorilla–man, or a dude, or a terror, or a romance. Just a first-class pugilist is not much use to the faithful . . . Carnera has to be at all costs the giant.'

The same review also quoted James R. Harrison of the New York *Morning Telegraph*: 'We have to admit that the Carnera person is something beyond a mere freak . . . He can move around with something more than elephantine grace and agility. He has a nice fighting style, squared off with both fists ready . . . [He] faces his man and plows ahead, fists swinging busily . . . With his size, his strength, and his comparative speed, Carnera has the greatest physical equipment that any heavyweight has ever been blessed with. Handled properly and given the necessary polishing, this marvellous equipment might be turned into a devastating force . . . Carnera ought to be the greatest drawing card since Jack Dempsey.'

Jeff Dickson, to whom Carnera owed the start of his professional career, had earned nothing from the American tour. There were no objections, therefore, from the boxer or his European manager, Léon Sée, when the Paris-based American promoter proposed rounding off the year with two genuine bouts, one in Barcelona against the European heavyweight champion, Paulino Uzcudun, the other against Reggie Meen in London. But before that, Carnera had some dates to keep in his own country, if only to prove how he had been robbed of victory in Boston and to expunge the memory of his shameful bout with Epifanio Islas in Milan two years earlier. He need not have worried about this. Thousands of his fellow-countrymen were there to cheer him when he disembarked from the *Conte Grande* at Genoa. Official greeters included representatives of the Italian Federation of Boxing, commanders of the Friuli fascist militia and the mayor of Sequals. From then until his departure for Barcelona, he was mobbed by both sexes, who broke through police cordons wherever he appeared, to plead for his autograph or simply to touch him. He had already agreed to attend a press reception in Rome, put on by the Federation, and on arriving at the capital the first official visitor to the hotel was the Federation's president, Raffaele Riccardi. The president was effusive with his welcome. The young Friulano boxer had brought glory to his country. The president was speaking for *il Duce*, Benito Mussolini, in wishing Primo all success and further glory on the road towards the world heavyweight championship. The great cities of Italy, north and south, were clamouring to do homage to their supreme gladiator of the ring, and it had been the Federation's privilege and pleasure to make that possible by arranging public exhibitions in Rome, Udine, Bologna and Milan. The inclusion of Udine was in recognition of the boxer's regional affiliation. Other cities were pleading to be favoured, but would have to accept disappointment in view of Primo's commitment in Barcelona. Before taking his leave, the president brought up one small and final detail. As the whole world knew, the great Primo Carnera had made a vast and well-deserved fortune for himself in the United States of America. There could be no doubt, therefore, that he would be the first to insist on waiving any fees or expenses in connection with his forthcoming triumphant tour of the nation that had given him birth.

Primo was already nodding and gesturing his consent. His French manager, after swallowing hard, fell in line. There was just one problem. The schedule fixed by Riccardi would be spread over twelve days, with the final exhibition falling in Milan on a Friday, just nine days before the fight in Barcelona. The next boat from Genoa to Barcelona sailed on the Monday, putting in at the Catalan port on the following day. This would leave too little time for Carnera to get into fighting trim, so perhaps the president would use his good offices to bring forward the date of the Milan exhibition. Riccardi regretted that it would not be possible to change the date at this short notice. But not to worry. He would arrange for an Italian Air Force plane to be put at their disposal. It would get them to Barcelona within a few hours of the exhibition in Milan.

The Rome exhibition went well, but the next one, in Udine's open-air stadium, was delayed a few days by torrential rainfall. It gave Carnera that much more time to be with his family in Sequals, and in the meanwhile Léon Sée was greatly relieved by an offer of 10,000 *lire* to give an exhibition in Florence, the day after the one scheduled for Bologna. This fee would just about cover the Carnera team's costs of inter-city travel, hotels and payments to local sparring partners, towards which the Federation was not contributing a cent. Sée told the Federation about the offer and no objection was raised.

On arrival in Bologna, Sée received a telephone call from Signore Massia, the secretary of the Federation of Boxing. He had bad news and good news to report. Bad news: the Air Force had refused to come up with a plane. Good news: the Milan exhibition would therefore be cancelled. A boat was sailing for Barcelona the morning following the Bologna exhibition, arriving a week before the Uzcudun fight. At this point, Sée reminded Massia that, as the Federation already knew, Carnera was under contract to give an exhibition next day – but in the evening – in Florence. Not to worry, said the secretary. Call them and tell them that it's cancelled, with the Federation's authority and consent. *Force majeure*.

So they cancelled Florence, sacrificed the fee and took the boat to Barcelona. A few weeks later, Carnera was formally notified by the Federation that he and Sée had been fined a thousand dollars between them for non-execution of the Florence contract. Until it was paid, the fine would be automatically increased by five thousand *lire* for every public bout he fought. Sée wrote to Mussolini, pointing out that Carnera had become French by naturalization after emigrating to France in 1922. He had never sought an Italian boxing licence and therefore could not be disciplined by the Federation. The letter was forwarded to Signore Riccardi, who confirmed in his reply that Carnera had not in fact applied for a licence. Out of the goodness of their heart, the Federation had made him a present of one, waiving the usual fee.

During his brief stay in Sequals, Primo had promised his

parents and his two brothers, 22-year-old Secondo and 18-year-old Severino, that he would come back to spend a few days before Christmas with them and added that he had plans to build a handsome house for himself in the little town, to which he would retire and live like a gentleman after he had become heavyweight champion of the world. He also confided to his brothers that he had an *inamorata* named Emilia in London and that he and she had been exchanging love letters throughout the year. He intended to marry her, but they were to keep this a secret from their mother until he was able to introduce his fiancée formally to the family, after his next tour of the USA.

There is no doubt that he sincerely intended marriage. In February of that year he had written: 'Emilia, my dearest little girl whom I love, I won my second fight here in America. You can live tranquilly because I will not have another girl but you. They are all aversion to me. They frighten me, all but you . . . . You will be my wife before a year.'★

And, with a remarkable show of vulnerability from a world celebrity writing to a young Soho waitress: 'My dearest Emilia for life, I cannot sleep at night. My thoughts are always with you because you can say you have taken the whole of my life. You should always be faithful to me. You should not forget me and go with another . . . A day will come when we shall no longer be separated . . . I do not think it is far distant . . . Have patience for another year and we shall be together for always.'

And again, in case her faith in him should flag: 'Emilia, my star, I never tire of reading your letters. I am up to my eyes in work. I could have a fight every day if I wanted it . . . I am earning a lot of money and am having tremendous success . . . One day I will be champion of the world. Have confidence in me, for this cursed year will pass quickly.'

There had not really been much time to get to know each other in London, that autumn and winter of 1929. What with training for his three fights at the Albert Hall, his variety engagement at the Alhambra and exhibitions away from the

★ All letters to Emilia were written in Italian.

capital, theirs had been a fragmented relationship, uncemented – or undermined – by sexual intercourse, which would have been unthinkable, anyway, between 'respectable' working-class Italian Catholics. When Primo wrote about being 'frightened' by American females, he would have been expressing his inability to cope, that first year, with the brazen provocation offered by these Amazons, whether out of curiosity or cupidity. Now he was back in Europe and eager to renew his courting of Emilia, after almost a year's separation. Her letters to him had been satisfyingly affectionate and understanding, as might be expected from someone raised in a culture that favoured longish engagements over rash gallops to the altar.

'My adored love, This morning I received your telegram saying that you won in three rounds. [v. Bertazzolo on 30 August] Bravo, my Primo. I am glad that your name does credit to our dear country and to your dear family and future wife. Another four months and I will then have you with me. What a joy when I think that soon I shall be able to see you and to have you in my arms and to have your longed-for kisses. It seems to me that I die of joy.'

Emilia did not even have to wait another four months after mailing that letter on 1 September. Somewhat to Léon Sée's annoyance, his English wife, Rosie, with whom Emilia had been corresponding, proposed giving their men a surprise by turning up in Barcelona for the Uzcudun fight. Apart from a brief, and, one imagines, emotional, reunion at the Hotel Oriente on the Ramblas, where Carnera was staying, the lovers were sternly separated by Sée and Dickson until after the bout, which was being bedevilled enough, without extraneous pressures. Paolino Uzcudun, 'The Bull of the Pyrenees', was a national hero to all the Spaniards. A one-time woodcutter in his native Basque country, he had taken the European heavyweight title from Erminio Spalla in 1926 and had subsequently spent two years in the United States, giving an impressive account of himself as a 'punching machine' against a series of strong opponents. He was now 32 years old and would be weighing in at 209 lb against Carnera's 258, but he would have virtually all of a 65,000 crowd at the Montjuich stadium yelling for him. The bout had been scheduled for 23 November, but a general strike closed down all transport throughout Spain and caused a postponement of the match. Meanwhile, the good Catalans of Barcelona, thousands of whom were daily paying to watch the giant Italian training at the Teatro Olimpia, were also confirming their political affinity with the Basques by jeering at Carnera every time he mixed it with one of his sparring partners. Fortunately for Jeff Dickson, who stood to make more money from this promotion than from any of his past ventures, the strike ended after a few days and the special trains, planes and buses were now disgorging their thousands of excited fight fans in good time for the opening of the stadium gates on 30 November.

At Sée's insistence, backed by Dickson, the Spanish boxing authorities had agreed to a neutral referee, an Englishman, plus two judges, one Spanish and one Italian. But the Catalans had kept a trick or two up their sleeves, as they showed when a dispute arose over the gloves Carnera was to wear for the fight. Under international rules, the gloves worn by heavyweight boxers must not weigh less than six ounces or more than ten, and most professionals obviously preferred to wear the regulation minimum. Carnera's closed fist measured 14¾ in, and for these abnormal hands Sée had gloves specially made, weighing sometimes up to eight or nine ounces. These permitted – even encouraged – Carnera to make a properly closed fist, something that did not come naturally to the giant boxer. For the Uzcudun fight, the Catalan authorities refused to let Carnera wear his usual gloves. Instead, they had two pairs made to their own specification, each glove weighing 7½ ounces and each with the same thickness of horsehair stuffing over the knuckles as would go into Uzcudun's. But when Carnera tried them on he found that one of the pairs prevented him from fully closing his fists. So he chose the other pair and the ever-vigilant Léon Sée took the precaution of making a pen mark on the gloves of his choice.

On the afternoon of the fight, when the sealed gloves were

brought to Carnera's dressing room, he found they had given him the wrong pair. He protested, but the Spaniards insisted it was the pair he had chosen, despite the non-existence of Sée's pen mark. And when he threatened to walk out of the stadium, he was accused of making an excuse so as to avoid being beaten by the Basque. The stadium was already filling up. Jeff Dickson, to whom Primo considered he owed so much, would be ruined if the fight were cancelled. It would take some guts to confront the Bull of the Pyrenees over ten rounds with half-open gloves, but Carnera finally elected to do just that. But not before Sée had secured, under threat of pulling out of the bout, a letter from the president of the Catalan boxing federation confirming that he had refused Carnera's request for a change of gloves, an admission that later brought him a reproof from the International Boxing Union.

Regardless of its outcome, Léon Sée's agreement to let the fight take place was an appalling act of betrayal and a callous exploitation by him and Jeff Dickson of their boxer's loyalty and courage. Uzcudun was no stylist but he had fought most of the world's best heavyweights and was the embodiment of animal energy with his bull neck, flat Basque face and iron-hard muscles. In height, he was conceding seven inches, which meant he would be working almost exclusively on Carnera's body rather than going for the eyes and chin. For the full ten rounds the Italian absorbed more body punishment than in all of his previous bouts put together, without being able to deliver any of the closed-fist blows that might have hurt his opponent. But he skilfully built up the points with his stabbing left, outlasted the Basque in wind and energy and was awarded the fight by a 2–1 verdict, with the Spanish judge predictably the odd man out.

Time would tell what lasting effect this rendezvous in Barcelona would have on Carnera's health. For the moment, he was more than content to have won recognition for the first time as the only credible European contender for the world title, and this just two years and three months after his début as a boxer. It was at this time that Max Schmeling, who had captured the vacant title in June of that year on a foul by the co-contender

Jack Sharkey, was being publicly criticized by Jack Dempsey for refusing to give Sharkey a return bout. As the Manassa Mauler put it, with an interesting blend of simile and metaphor, 'He has closed himself up like an oyster in its shell and flown with his crown to Germany where he is treasuring it jealously.' Carnera was not exactly treading on the Teutonic monarch's train, but he was catching up. A New York newspaper, *The Sun*, reporting the results of a referendum among seventy American boxing critics, listed the Italian as fourth in the rank of world heavyweights. Ahead of him in the critics' estimation were only Stribling, Sharkey and Schmeling. After him came Griffith, Godfrey, Campolo, Loughran, Baer and Risko.

The reunion in Barcelona between Carnera and his sweetheart Emilia Tersini was short in duration and no doubt greatly exciting for them both. But if Emilia had set out from London in the hope that Primo might now be ready to set a date for their marriage, she was disappointed. Earlier that year, he had written to her from Los Angeles, after disposing of the black boxer Neil Clisby in two rounds: 'Now, my treasure, do you know that here I am the most popular man in the world? The day before yesterday I received an engagement from Hollywood to make a film with Lon Chaney. In November I shall make a tour of Europe, and thus we shall see if I can get married at once, or wait a little while.'

The letter, with its totally uncharacteristic boastfulness, revealed a naïve and pathetic eagerness to impress his loved one and keep her in thrall. His 'we shall see' reference to an immediate marriage might have sent Emilia's hopes soaring, but it was an essentially hollow attempt at assurance. He would have been as ready to wed as she was. But he was well aware that the decision would not be his but his managers', none of whom had the slightest intention at this stage of letting the golden eggs from their oversized goose drop into a conjugal nest. Just how dependent Carnera was made to feel upon Sée had been shown in another letter to Emilia, couched in terms that could hardly have put her in a fever of anticipatory joy: 'My much desired wife, My manager tells me that when we are married we will make a tour of the world with him and his wife. Thus, we shall be quite alone [*sic*] and able to do everything you like. We shall also be able to see my dear papa and mama.'

Despite Primo's protestations of fidelity, it would have been remarkable had Emilia not been concerned that the young boxer who had wooed her a year ago in London would be stolen from her by some blonde Yankee glamour-puss now that his fame had spread across two continents. So far, he had given her no cause for anxiety about this. Indeed, if there was any lack of trust between them, it seemed to lurk in his mind rather than hers. She had still been working as a waitress at Molinari's in May of that year when Primo wrote to say he would like her to give up her job, 'The work is too hard for you.' Knowing the nature of her male compatriots, Emilia would not have been deceived. Hard work – *niente*! Where had Primo first met her and chatted her up but in the free-and-easy atmosphere of a Soho restaurant? Dutifully, she reported she had quit Molinari's and gone to work in a restaurant managed by one of her uncles. But this was also in the wicked square mile of Soho and the work would still be 'too hard' for her. He had never sent her money and she could not sponge off her parents, so she took a job in a London department store, working eight hours a day for fifteen shillings a week. As a waitress she has been earning £3 to £4 a week, with tips.

Emilia need not have been unduly upset by the fact that Carnera did not take her with him on his brief trip to Sequals after the Uzcudun fight. As from 19 December, when he would meet Reggie Meen in London's Albert Hall, he was contracted all the way through the first month of 1931 to give exhibitions in England, Scotland and Scandinavia. It was bad enough not to be able to spend the actual Christmas days with his family. To descend on his mother with a totally strange young woman in tow would hardly make for the most comfortable of home-comings. To Emilia, the fact that she was soon to see her *fidanzato* again in London would probably have been poor consolation, however, knowing she would be sharing him with hordes of journalists, photographers and fight fans. But she had Primo's promise that he would tell his mother all about her and that this was the last time he would be going home without his dearest Emilia at his side.

The 'victorious' American tour, followed by the genuine defeat of the redoubtable Paolino Uzcudun, had further boosted Carnera's stock in Britain where, as in the USA, much of the attraction of heavyweight contests had been weakened by the retirement of Dempsey and Tunney. The Italian giant was giving the boxing fans what Maurice Chevalier was currently dispensing to London music-hall audiences: a novel and exotic infusion of entertainment values. Reggie Meen, just 22 years old, 6 ft 3 in. tall and weighing in at 220 lb, was hardly in the same league as Uzcudun and the fight was stopped in Carnera's favour in the second round by a justifiably concerned referee. There had been letters to the British press calling for cancellation of the fight on the grounds that it was a travesty to put any normal human being up against the giant Italian. Trevor Wignall, Primo's best friend among the boxing critics, seemed almost to be on the side of the protesters when he wrote:

> When Carnera removed his gown . . . there were gasps of astonishment all around where I was sitting. His phenomenal chest and arms were the things that produced the astonishment.
>
> The man is much more than a 'normal abnormal', as he was once described to me by a doctor. Professional boxing has never known anyone like him. Most certainly he is a giant, but he is also a giant who is most marvellously equipped both mentally and physically. Any present day fighter who is matched to meet him is going to look an infant by comparison, and I cannot help but think that the day is rapidly approaching when it will be found impossible to get opponents for him, except perhaps in exhibitions.*

* *Daily Express*, 20 December 1930.

There were plenty of these over the next two months. It was just as well, for America's NBA, in support of the Italian Federation of Boxing, had barred Carnera from all rings under its aegis and he was also being barred by several states outside the NBA jurisdiction. The exhibitions served to bolster Carnera's morale as well as the bank accounts of Léon Sée and Jeff Dickson who, between them, could pocket 45 per cent of the money rolling in before deducting their and Carnera's expenses. If 10 per cent of the gross receipts was left for the star of these shows, he could have counted himself fortunate. But wherever he appeared, throughout Britain, Denmark and Sweden, the people turned out in their welcoming thousands to see him in the flesh and to pack the local music-halls where the Man Mountain sparred with the biggest of the local heavyweights and performed his physical exercises. No prize-fighter at any time had put on so many public exhibitions over so short a period.

But this was still only the start of 1931 and exhibitions, however lucrative, were just a marking of time until the Italian could return to America and win the right to challenge for the world title. Meanwhile, the title itself had become a bone of bitter dispute between the NYSAC and the NBA. The New York authority was insisting that Jack Sharkey should be recognized by default as the world champion if the title-holder Max Schmeling refused to give him a return match that summer – in Madison Square Garden, of course. The NBA was insisting that Stribling ranked ahead of Sharkey in the order of contenders and should therefore have first crack at the title. In the end, the NBA got their way and a date was set in July for the German and Stribling to do battle in Cleveland, Ohio, a state that had all along recognized Schmeling as the only legitimate champion. As part of the contract, the winner would defend his title against Primo Carnera later that year. No one seems to have wondered at the time how and where either of the two parties to the contract were to meet in combat with a boxer banned from fighting in New York and most other states of the Union. The intention, perhaps, was to leave this minor issue to be addressed next time the members of the two powerful authorities were running short of reasons to pick up their *per diem* envelopes.

In the meantime, Carnera was now a recognized contender for the world championship, and his 'syndicate' of managers – still including Léon Sée – decided the time had come for him to return to the USA and put right the wrong that was done to him by the referee of his bout with Jim Maloney. The Bostonian had agreed to come to Miami for the fight on 5 March, but the benefit to Carnera of this neutral locale was outweighed on the night by some bad luck for the Italian during training, when he had a rib cracked by a hard-punching sparring partner, Walter Cobb. The request for a postponement of the fight was rejected by the local boxing commissioners and Carnera had to fight with part of his chest in plaster and bandaged.

There was emotional stress on top of this. In London, upon his return from Sequals, Carnera had again been pressed by Emilia about marriage. In response to his pleas, she had agreed to be patient for another six months or so, but as the new year unfolded and Primo's replies to her flow of love letters were cut by travel and training, a note of reproach began to be sounded from London: 'Have you not found a minute to write to me? Oh, Primo, why do you wish to make me suffer so much? Believe me, I do not deserve it, you have all my life, all my love. Primo, my angel, be good.'

Her angel had responded to this *cri de coeur*, a few days before the Maloney fight, with a letter that carried its own reproach, together with more than a touch of injured pride, overlaying guilt: 'I know that I am very bad, but what would you have? It is not my fault. If you suffer, I too suffer . . . I urge you, Emilia mine, not to worry and not to have ugly thoughts, because when I say one thing I do not say another, and you will know that my word is golden and it is worth more than any contract.'

What with the cracked rib and the emotional upset, it was perhaps surprising that he even went the full ten rounds with Jim Maloney, leave alone being awarded the fight on points – a decision that brought whistles and boos from a bored turnout of 20,000 spectators, hardly enough of them to offset the promoters' costs. The truth of the matter, however, as shown by the preceding bouts with Maloney, Uzcudun and Meen, was that the Italian boxer was still not punching his weight. To do this, he would have to *want* to wreak damage on his opponent. He would have to find a way of climbing into the ring with violence on his mind and unreined power in his fists. It meant he would first have to generate something like a cold hatred for the 'enemy' in the opposite corner; and the hail-fellow-well-met Primo, the giant who liked to laugh and be liked, had not been able to turn that emotion on to order.

The Miami fight did little to raise his status as a contender. Nor did the series of six genuine knockout victories over non-ranking opponents that followed during the summer. In the meanwhile, nevertheless, the NYSAC reinstated him for a bout against Jack Sharkey, to be staged at Ebbet's Field, Brooklyn, and had declared, to the intense annoyance of their erstwhile pals at Madison Square Garden, that this would be for the world title. Now the lawyers for the Garden stepped in. They sued the NYSAC and its chairman, James A. Farley, in the federal court and won an injunction against a Sharkey–Carnera championship match. Meanwhile, the Garden had failed to prevent the NBA-backed title fight between Schmeling and Stribling at Cleveland on 3 July when, against most predictions, the German won by a technical knockout, punching the American challenger to a standstill in the fourteenth round.

Carnera, who had watched the fight from the ringside in company with the great Gene Tunney and the legendary former champion Jim Corbett, could now prepare himself for the promised title fight later that year and the realization of Léon Sée's Great Idea, two years ahead of the Frenchman's most optimistic schedule. But their excitement was shortlived. From Paris, where Schmeling had hastened after the fight, came the news that one of his eyes was still seriously affected from its meeting with Stribling's thumb in the course of the first round. His doctor had ordered four months' rest from prize-fighting. Depressing as this must have been to the Carnera camp, it was welcome news to the moguls of US boxing. A world title bout

between two non-American pugilists would have been about as
attractive to New Yorkers as a soccer match between Blackburn
Rovers and Tottenham Hotspurs. There were suggestions by
the press that the German hadn't the slightest wish to meet
either Carnera or Sharkey, except maybe over a nice glass of
schnapps, and his failure to rendezvous with the Italian lent
force to the Garden's argument that Sharkey should be
regarded as the *de facto* champion and that there could be no
recognition of a *de jure* champion who had not first challenged
and beaten him.

The first challenge came from a former world middleweight
champion, the great Mickey Walker, who proceeded on 22 July
at the Garden to give Sharkey a lesson in boxing, over the
distance. He was clearly the victor; when the verdict was
announced in Sharkey's favour, the booing that went up from
the spectators ought to have been disturbing enough to the
judges without the loud raspberry from a ringside observer
named Al Capone. But how else could the judges have acted?
Someone would have to take the *de jure* title from the German
and bring it back to where it belonged, in the USA, and Sharkey
– or Coccosky, to give him his Lithuanian family name – was the
guy the boys were banking on to do it.

Stribling's defeat by Schmeling had moved Carnera up in the
short list of contenders. Only Sharkey now stood between him
and the official or unofficial title. In the light of Sharkey's
unconvincing showing against Walker, the Italian's managers
deemed it reasonably safe to put their man up against the
ex-sailor, and the bout was set for 12 October.

On the face of it, there was the promise of a good fight.
Sharkey would be giving away fifty-six pounds and almost
seven inches in height; against this there was the 30-year-old
Bostonian's record of forty-seven fights over nine years, in the
course of which he had defeated such top-ranking opponents as
Jim Maloney, Johnny Risko, Young Stribling and George
Godfrey, as well as lasting seven rounds in 1927 against the great
Jack Dempsey, who afterwards acknowledged that 'Sharkey
gave me living hell for the first five rounds and was as good a

fighter as I have ever seen.'

Born at the turn of the century of immigrant Lithuanian parents, Sharkey joined the US Navy at eighteen and after six years' service started straight in as a professional boxer. Unlike Carnera and so many other exploited prize-fighters, he had kept a shrewd eye on the money side of his career. By 1931 he was one of the richest boxers in the game, having kept most of the million dollars he had earned up until then.

Whether from his early years in the navy, his Lithuanian blood, or a combination of the two influences, his temperament was at variance with what might have been expected in a heavyweight pugilist. For one thing, he could burst into tears upon such little provocation, for example, as a fervent rendering of 'God Bless America' or the Lithuanian national anthem, whatever it was at that time. And in the course of a fight he might suddenly be seized by an impulse to dance up and down the ring, using steps vaguely suggestive of a hornpipe crossed with a Highland fling. Such eccentricities apart, he was up there with the most aggressive fighters in the heavyweight class, though considered by some critics, at the time, to have started on the slow way down.

Public interest in Sharkey v. Carnera was not exactly at fever pitch, and only 40,000 customers turned up on the night. They were given terrific value for their money. Neither of the contestants held anything back, from start to finish, and each exhibited in full measure those qualities of guts and endurance that typify boxing at its best. Despite an early knockdown, Carnera was probably slightly ahead on points over the first nine rounds. It had been a stunning left hook to the chin that had put him on his back in the fourth round. As the count started, he raised himself to one knee, looking towards his corner for confirmation that he should profit from the New York State rule allowing a fighter to take up to a count of nine in that position. But with Léon Sée signalling to him to fight on and Bill Duffy waving him to stay down, the Italian started uncertainly to rise. When Sharkey made to pounce on him from a neutral corner, Carnera lowered himself again to one knee and took the count to nine, while Sharkey protested vainly. Now the Italian took the fight to the ex-sailor until the ninth round, when another terrific hook to the chin shook him badly. He had been using his long left jab to reduce the toll of Sharkey's punishing in-fighting, but the arm was tiring by the eleventh round when Sharkey began to weave in and hammer away with both fists. From there until the bell sounded for the end of the fifteenth, with a fund of courage that impressed even the hardboiled New York sports writers, Carnera endured what he afterwards spoke of as 'the worst thrashing I shall ever expect to get'. There was no dispute about the points victory awarded to Sharkey, only praise for the brave performance by both fighters. A *Daily Express* editorial, two days later, said it all:

> Heavyweight boxing badly needed such a fight . . . The world had grown sceptical of men of their bulk really hitting one another or of any fight going fifteen rounds. But Sharkey and Carnera . . . battered one another ferociously, mercilessly, with all the punishment-taking pluck of the old-time bruisers, for fifteen gruelling rounds. Sharkey won, but as an exhibition of physical vigour and gameness the honours were even. It is now possible to speak of heavyweight prize-fighting without a yawn.

The object of Carnera's greatest pride during this second tour of America was the gleaming Chrysler Imperial limousine he now owned and was in the habit of driving with all the reckless bravura of an Italian male who had never owned even a bicycle of his own. There had already been some close scrapes on the road with Primo at the wheel – enough for Léon Sée to have insisted that their Japanese chauffeur, Henry, should drive them to and from the training camp at Orangeburg during the weeks leading up to the Sharkey fight. Henry had a full passenger complement when he set out for New York City two days before the bout. Apart from a journalist working on pre-fight stories, there was Carnera seated at the back between Léon Sée and Maurice Eudeline, and one of Sée's sons on a jump seat, facing them. Responding to Primo's call for more speed, Henry stepped on the pedal at the precise moment when a Cadillac shot a traffic light at an intersection just coming up. There was a head-on crash, shooting the passengers in the Chrysler out of their seats. One of the journalists suffered a scalp wound. Part of the force of Carnera's plunge was absorbed by Sée's son. But when Sée and the others recovered from the shock they found Carnera in a semi-conscious daze from the impact of his head against the jump seat's hard padding.

The immediate fear, of course, was that the Sharkey fight might have to be postponed, with all the problems that would incur. Carnera was helped into the back room of a nearby gas station where he remained for about half an hour, getting over the experience. There were no outward signs of injury and the journalist agreed, under coaxing by Sée, that there was no great story to report. Nevertheless, Carnera was almost certainly suffering some effect from the accident when he went into the ring with Sharkey, and it is to his credit and Sée's that they made no mention of it until much later, and then in no way as an excuse for the defeat of 12 October.

The fact remained: Primo Carnera had been given a chance to leapfrog Sharkey in the contender stakes and had failed. He was now, at 25, back to being one of a handful of heavyweights lined up for future cracks at the title. There is no evidence that he was deeply dispirited by this or ever in any real doubt about winning the championship. With Léon Sée, it was another story. He had penetrated the clouds veiling the summit of his Great Idea, but was now back again in their enveloping swirl. There would be no return bout with Sharkey until after Schmeling decided to defend his title, which would not be until some time in 1932. The educated 52-year-old Frenchman was increasingly unhappy in his relationship with Duffy, Madden and their semi-literate hangers-on. Early in the 1930 tour of America, he had sent for his wife Rosie and three of their children and installed them in a rented bungalow at Atlantic Beach. This had provided a pleasant refuge, between fight dates, from the banalities and vulgarities of the 'syndicate's' West Side milieu and Primo had enjoyed his visits to the beach and romping with Léon's two daughters, Quinny and Pauline. None of the family had wanted to return to the States for the second year and the father was missing them and Paris more than he had expected to. On top of all this, Jeff Dickson had been pressing him to bring Primo back to Europe for a series of lucrative bouts and exhibitions, from which he and Léon would be the exclusive beneficiaries, now that he, Dickson, had bought out Paul Journée's interest for 240,000 francs, the rough equivalent then of £3,000.

And now Primo himself was pressing to be allowed to celebrate Christmas in Sequals. He had promised Emilia that they would spend the holiday there with his family. His 23-year-old brother Secondo, who was now working in London, would accompany her on the trip.

There remained two dates in the 1931 calendar: a rendezvous with King Levinsky in Chicago on 19 November and a meeting with the Argentinian heavyweight champion Vittorio Campolo at Madison Square Garden eight days later. They would be genuine fights against tough opponents. Levinsky, four years younger than Carnera, had already won against Jim Maloney by a knockout, and it took Carnera a full ten rounds to gain his points decision. Campolo got shorter shrift. He weighed 220 pounds and stood 6 ft 4 in. tall. He also had a big mouth, which he had been using before the fight to boast of how he would disgrace the Italian in the eyes of his New York *compatrioti*. He ought to have known better than to affront his opponent's patriotic sensibilities. A grim-faced Carnera put the Argentinian down for a count of nine in the second round, with a left hook. Campolo got up, only to hit the canvas again on receipt of a right hook, and stay put for the full count. It was probably just as well that the fight ended there. For the first time in his boxing career, Carnera had entered the ring angry. He had meant to hit Campolo hard. If the blows did not have his full weight behind them that night it was only because he had not yet, and never would, master the technique of combining accuracy with crispness of delivery and concentrated power. But even at half-strength, with anger driving them, a few more hooks and uppercuts might have caused Campolo far more serious discomfort than that which went with the swallowing of his insults.

There was the usual cable of congratulations from Emilia on Carnera's breakfast table at the Hotel Victoria next day. It also thanked him for the $250 he had sent to cover the expenses of her Christmas journey to Sequals. It was the first time he had ever given money to a woman, apart from the monthly remittances he made to his mother. There were payments, of course, to the girls supplied for his pleasure after the fights, but this was taken care of either by M'sieur Sée or Mr Duffy. He assumed, correctly, that it would be put down to his account with the syndicate.

Sometimes – but much less often – he was allowed to take up an amateur's unsolicited offer.

6

Thrown to the Wolves

In his book, *Le Mystère Carnera*, Léon Sée listed the four distinct categories of women he had to deal with in his role as mentor and protector of Primo Carnera. First came the usual amateur gold-diggers with an eye on any celebrity, tall or short, slim or fat, with money to spread around. Even if they managed to get close to the boxer, they soon drifted away in search of prey with something more than pocket money at his immediate disposal.

Next came the movie or theatre actresses, often celebrities themselves, who were more than willing to share the flash-lights that bounced off the Italian at any social function he attended. To be featured next day in the press on the arm of the Ambling Alp was akin to being photographed with rifle in hand and a foot planted on the head of a Bengal tiger. It did not necessarily imply that one had done the full Delilah bit on the big lug. *Honi soit qui mal y pense*, and all that.

Third on Sée's list were what he described as *calculatrices . . . qui ne reculent pas devant un chantage bien conçu*, loosely translatable as 'operators not above a nice spot of blackmail'. And finally there were those whose interest stemmed from lubricious curiosity . . .

The publicity limelight-sharers were not unwelcome; indeed it was of mutual benefit for the smiling young pugilist to be photographed, in his sartorial elegance, escorting a beautiful actress to a movie première. To the pure at heart, the picture spoke of the freemasonry of the famous. In others, it provoked a thrill of voluptuous awe, as disturbing and acceptable as the legend of Beauty and the Beast.

The gold-diggers quickly tired of digging their infertile pits. The female blackmailers were always around, circling like hyenas and usually balked of their prey only by the unresting and wary vigilance of Léon Sée. Their plotting matched the crudeness of their natures. At its simplest, it could be a matter of flattering Carnera into giving a girl a run in his Chrysler Imperial and challenging him with, 'Faster, Primo!' in the hope of causing a minor collision from which she would incur 'internal injuries'. After the first of such try-ons, Sée proposed that the girl should either agree to be hospitalized in a private room at Carnera's expense and under the care of reputable specialists, or else get the hell out of it. It was the last they heard from her. Another fairly common ploy that might have paid off but for the quick thinking of the Frenchman was tried during the first year's tour of the States.

On arrival at the San Francisco hotel where bookings had been made for the entourage, Sée was slightly troubled by the fact that the room allotted to Carnera was on a different floor from the rest of the team's accommodation instead of right next to his own, which was how he liked it to be. He accepted the management's explanation for this and while the team's bags were taken up to the rooms they sat down in the restaurant for a meal. After a minute or two, Carnera became concerned about whether the bell-boys had understood that his baggage was to be separated from the rest. Léon Sée decided to go with him upstairs, just to check on his accommodation. Having collected the boxer's room key from the desk, Sée was a step ahead of him when he opened the bedroom door and walked in. Two young women rose from the king-size bed specially installed, as usual, for Carnera. One of them, with tousled hair, was wearing only camiknickers, ripped down the front. Her companion, the key witness to her distressed condition, was fully dressed. As Sée's mouth opened to apologize for entering the wrong room, he spotted Carnera's luggage stacked by the wall and in that same instant he threw himself back against the boxer and slammed the door shut. A call from the telephone in the corridor brought the house detective swiftly to the scene. When Carnera declined to press charges, the girls were given the bum's rush, with nothing to show for their trouble but torn camiknickers.

In a distinct and far less threatening category were the women – and they were legion, according to Sée – who wanted to find out for themselves if Primo Carnera's penis was proportionate to the rest of his body. Such women were rarely less than thirty years old and their initial approach to the research would usually be tentative and discreet. It might take the form of a request for an exclusive interview 'for my local newspaper' (unidentified) or a written invitation to tea when the boxer next found himself in their part of the world. Bolder spirits among them might make their pitch to the manager rather than directly to the object of their curiosity, and Sée treated us to the text of a typical letter from such a source:

Dear Sir, Knowing you to be a gentleman as well as a man of the world, I write in the conviction that you will treat this letter as strictly private and confidential. Would you be willing to grant me the great favour of an introduction to your fascinating friend and colleague Carnera, next time you are in this town or anywhere near it? I have a private income, am in perfect health, a great admirer of physical excellence and would be happy to send you a photograph of myself. I do so hope Primo will find it possible to take a short break from his busy life at his own convenience, and you may assure him that once he has made this dream of mine come true, I will keep secret whatever happens between us for ever.

Sée insists that he made a point of never answering the hundreds of such letters addressed to him. And he adds: 'Primo himself must also have received plenty. Was he in the habit of satisfying the senders' curiosity? I don't know. My contract as manager provided me with no percentage share in such peripheral perks.'

However, he made no attempt to hide the fact that Primo was a big boy now in more than the obvious sense, with certain appetites, other than gastronomic, to which he, as the fighter's manager and guardian, could not remain insensible. This was amusingly illustrated in that part of Sée's published testament dealing with the harassments that plagued them during their 1931 tour of the United States.

There had been so many unscrupulous attempts by lawyers and their clients to get their hands on Carnera's earnings that by November of that year Sée was in the habit of legally assigning to a third party, in advance, the purse money due from a promoter. This had been done before they arrived in Chicago for the Levinsky fight, but no one had mentioned that under Illinois state laws a foreigner could be put under 'preventative arrest' merely upon a declaration by a self-styled creditor. No fewer than four Chicago cops were waiting outside Carnera's dressing room on the night of 19 November when he made his way back from the ring after his win over King Levinsky. He and Sée were informed of a claim against them that was totally spurious, as would be proved in the court next day. Meanwhile, however, they would be detained under preventative arrest in the local jail. Léon Sée had been long enough in America to know that there was always a way to cushion the rigours of arrest and detention. A quiet word with the leader of the squad, and an understanding was reached. The two accused could be detained in their own hotel suite. The cops would spend the night in the sitting room between the two bedrooms separately occupied by the fighter and his manager. Bootleg whiskey would of course be laid on, to sustain the cops in their vigil, and they would not mind if Primo retired early with the female companion already booked as his reward for a hard evening's work in the ring.

The arrangement seemed to be working out smoothly enough, with Sée in his room, making phone calls, the cops in theirs, playing poker, and Carnera closeted in his bedroom, enjoying his reward. But a report had gone out that the boxer had been arrested and locked up. Failing to find him in the jailhouse, a snoop of reporters and photographers had turned up at the hotel and were now outside the sitting-room door to the suite, clamouring to be let in. The cops had no intention of sharing their hooch with the press, and to Léon Sée the prospect of having Primo photographed *in flagrante delicto* was equally unwelcome. Opening the sitting-room door just a fraction, he told the pressmen that Carnera was sound asleep, must not be disturbed, and would be available for questions and pictures in the morning. An agitated spokesman for the Fourth Estate tried to explain why the mighty rotary printing machines could not remain stilled and silent until the Ambling Alp had his coffee and doughnuts; and when the little manager responded with a Gallic shrug, the boys started confidently to push their way in. This was when the four cops, alarmed by the way things were going, moved swiftly and silently to Sée's assistance and provided the backup – unseen by the press – of their shoulders to the inside of the door. To the pressmen, the speed and violence with which they were hurled back by the slamming door could have only one explanation: the giant Italian pugilist was inside the room and in a dangerously hostile mood. It seemed a convenient time to take a powder.

That an unmarried prize-fighter might make use of call-girls during a tour of the United States can hardly in itself raise other than an unworldly or puritanical eyebrow. When Carnera told Emilia, in one of his first letters from America, that the American women frightened him and were 'all aversion to me', he was no doubt telling her the truth at the time, about the women he had met socially. Most European males of the era, exposed for the first time to the guileless and extroverted North American female, would be at a loss to know how to deal with her after a lifetime spent with relatively unassertive European women. Carnera, the uneducated country hick turned fairground freak turned prize-fighter, would have been no exception. At the same time, he had all the psycho-physical needs of a young and healthy man for sexual expression, with nothing standing in his way except his pledge of fidelity to Emilia Tersini ('I will not have another girl but you'). But if Emilia truly believed that her Italian lover would be capable of resisting any female challenge,

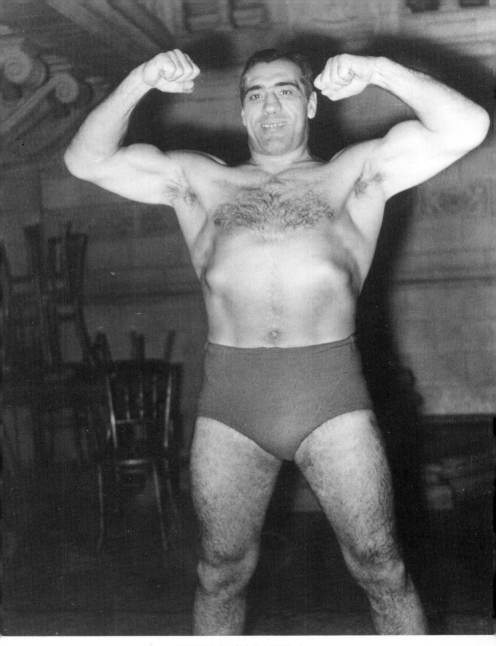

PRIMO CARNERA
born 25 October 1906   died 19 June 1967
The eleventh world champion of gloved heavyweight boxing
and the first and only Italian ever to have held the title.
(S&G Press Agency Ltd)

From his first unbroken series of victories in France, the 23-year-old Primo Carnera arrives in London for his October 1929 debut at the Royal Albert Hall. The triple handshake includes his opponent, the British heavyweight, Jack Stanley, and *(centre)* the Paris-based promoter, Jefferson Dickson. *(S&G Press Agency Ltd)*

(left) Emilia Tersini, the Soho waitress who would successfully sue Carnera for breach of promise in 1933. *(UPI/ Bettmann)*

Manager Léon Sée *(seated right)* signs him up for his first bout in the USA with six-foot-four 'Big Boy' Peterson. Co-managers Bill Duffy and Luigi Soresi are to Carnera's right and left.
(AP Wide World Photos)

'. . . and the new heavyweight champion of the world . . .' Carnera exults before stunned ringsiders at the Long Island Bowl while anxious seconds attend to dethroned Jack Sharkey.
(AP Wide World Photos)

Back home in Sequals on the patio of his favourite bar, Primo dispenses wine to (*left to right*) his brother Severino, his mother Giovanna and his father Sante. (*AP Wide World Photos*)

(*left*) Based now in Los Angeles, Carnera enjoys, between wrestling engagements, a second career as a screen actor, featured with such stars as Bob Hope, Marlon Brando, Janet Leigh and (*here*) Britain's Audrey Dalton. (*UPI/ Bettmann*)

On the set of a Hollywood film studio, the new world champion co-stars with Myrna Loy and Max Baer in the film, *The Prizefighter and the Lady*. Shortly after the release of this movie, Carnera and Baer would fight for real in the Madison Square Bowl on Long Island. *(UPI/Bettmann)*

Primo's marriage on the eve of World War Two to Giuseppina Kovacic was the prelude to years of austerity behind the Axis lines. *(AP Wide World Photos)*

In 1950, an exasperated referee – none other than Jack Dempsey – throws a punch at Carnera for ignoring his cautions. The younger of the two former world boxing champions easily slips the Manassa Mauler's right. *(UPI/Bettmann)*

United States citizens all! A late 1950s group photograph of teenagers Umberto and Jean with their mother and father.

On his last journey home to Sequals and the final count, the desperately ill and emaciated giant can still raise a feeble salute for his sorrowing fellow-countrymen. (*AP Wide World Photos*)

(*below*) They came to Sequals from far and wide to pay their last respects to the gentle giant who, thirty years earlier, had brought the greatest prize in the world of sport to Italy. Leading mourners (*bottom corner, right*) include Italy's world middleweight boxing champion, Nino Benvenuti, who carries Primo's jewel-encrusted championship belt.

however seductive, to his celibacy during the year they would be spending apart, she would have been living in cloud-cuckoo-land, and there is no evidence she was as naïve as that. She did, however, accept as absolutely sincere his reiterated promises to marry her, as in his letter of May 1931: 'You are always my coming true wife. Don't think I will leave you for another. I am going to give you a good piece of news. In August or September, I shall return home, and I want you to go to my home and wait there for me with my parents.'

At the time of his writing that letter, the October match against Sharkey had yet to be fixed. Nor had the vexed issue of his nationality arisen, to cause him and his managers to think twice about the wisdom of an early return to Europe. The bugbear was military service, compulsory in France and Italy, and the boxer's liability in one or the other nation. The complication arose from the fact that one of his early employers in France, before he was taken on by Paul Journée, had given him some papers to sign to avoid being repatriated to Italy. It turned out that these had been naturalization papers, making him a French citizen for the purpose of military service. He claimed not to have realized this at the time, and there is little doubt that had he remained just another itinerant worker the French army would have managed somehow to get along without him. As matters stood, a warrant for his arrest had been issued in June 1931 upon the expiry of the six months' grace allowed any French citizen who happened to be out of the country when the call-up papers arrived. Failure to report to the authorities after that would incur up to a year's imprisonment.

Carnera could see no advantage in being a French citizen, even if spared military service on the grounds of his flat feet and varicose veins. The French press – at least those sections of it that interested themselves in the matter – were taking the line that if Primo preferred being Italian that was all right with a public 'sporty enough to love a champion, whatever his nationality'. It seemed that the French consul in New York also took this view, following an interview with the boxer; and early in December, as the threat of military service in France

appeared to be lifting, Carnera embarked for Italy in the liner
Roma, all set for Christmas with the family in Sequals and the
announcement of his forthcoming marriage in London to
Emilia. With hindsight, he might have been wiser to reverse the
planned sequence of events. Emilia was made welcome when
she joined her lover in the family home at 52 Via Gian
Domenico Facchina. (The street was named after the master
mosaicist whose exquisite works adorn the churches and palaces
of so many of the world's capital cities.) After a few days in
Sequals, something turned sour in the relationship between
Giovanna Carnera and her prospective daughter-in-law. Emilia
would naturally have sought diligently to avoid antagonizing, by
word or deed, the matriarch of the family, but it wouldn't have
needed much to turn the 53-year-old Giovanna against this
London-born chit of a girl who could not even understand,
leave alone speak, the Friulano dialect. An off-the-cuff
reference, perhaps, to the beautiful little house Primo said he
was having specially built for her in California? An offer to cook
for Primo his favourite meal from the menu of Soho's Molinari
restaurant – a dish his mother had never even heard of? The very
fact – perhaps not properly taken in by Giovanna until now –
that Emilia had been a waitress in that notoriously ill-famed
quartier of London? Whatever it was, the feelings between the
two women became so strained that, once Christmas was over,
Primo persuaded Emilia to return at once to London. He would
join her there from Paris, immediately after a bout with Moise
Bouquillon in Paris, where Dickson had already negotiated his
exemption from military service.

But first, the matter of his nationality would have to be
settled, once and for all. Lawyers in Rome had already prepared
the necessary papers, and in the course of a forty-eight hour trip
to the capital, Carnera was able to re-establish his Italian
citizenship.

There was a price to pay, and the least of it was a settlement of
the outstanding fine imposed by the Federation of Italian
Boxing over the cancelled exhibition in Florence back in
November 1930. In addition, he was 'invited' by the President

of the Federation to make a promise that when he finally became the world heavyweight champion – which Signore Riccardi was confident would soon be the case – his first defence of the title would take place in the Eternal City of Rome. Oh, and just one more favour . . . It would be a superb gesture, vastly to be appreciated by the Federation, the party and the government, not to mention *il Duce* himself, if Carnera would agree to have his purse from this first title defence shared among the Fascist Party's approved athletic clubs and associations.

At this point, Sée and Carnera must surely have exchanged anguished glances. It was one thing to commit themselves, recklessly, to the venue for an as yet hypothetical bout. To agree to sacrifice the prize money from a first title defence – usually one of the biggest purses a new champion could look forward to – was something else. It must have been at this point that the president played his trump card. Oh, yes, on the question of military service, now that Primo's Italian citizenship was confirmed . . . Riccardi felt reasonably confident that, given the boxer's generous acceptance of his proposals, this patriotic duty could be discharged by his enrolment, merely on paper, of course, in one of the Blackshirt militia forces.

From Paris, where he stopped Bouquillon in two rounds with a technical knockout, Carnera moved up to Berlin to dispose of Ernst Guehring within five rounds, and then back to Paris to meet and outpoint the Belgian heavyweight champion of Europe, Pierre Charles, over ten rounds. The unfortunate Emilia, having heard nothing in the meanwhile from her *fidanzato*, had turned up in Berlin and, failing to get to Primo, had followed him to Paris where she was able to corner him in his hotel. According to her later testimony in court, this was when the boxer told her that his mother was totally opposed to the marriage. She considered Emilia's 'standing and character' to be incompatible with her son's position in life and temperament. However, Primo must have held out some hope for the young woman, for she returned quietly to London to await his arrival for a March engagement at the Albert Hall, instead of going for his eyes with a hat pin. She would of course have appreciated the power wielded by a strong-minded Italian mother over her doting sons, but was perhaps hoping that a reunion in London, where their romance had begun, would put Primo back on the marriage track.

It was a vain hope. She wrote to him from London, 'in piteous terms', as her counsel would subsequently and poignantly put it, but he ignored the letter. In London in March he managed to keep his distance from Emilia except for an evening when she tracked him down to a dance hall in Tottenham Court Road and, to her distress and chagrin, was completely snubbed. It seemed hardly the kind of behaviour one would have expected from the man whose head was then being modelled in bronze by Edward Merritt, who proclaimed it 'the most interesting male head I have ever sculpted ... It has strength, intelligence and, strangely enough, gentleness.' The gentleness would in fact always be there, as the natural concomitant of his gigantism; what was waning was the sunny optimism about his future and the self-confidence this had engendered. Jeff Dickson was staging two fights for Carnera in the Albert Hall: a second encounter with George Cook, who had been knocked out by the Italian in Cleveland in July 1930, and then a bout with the white South African, Don McCorkindale. Neither of these opponents was of the status that could possibly enhance Carnera's image as a ranking contender for the world title.

And now a deep sense of guilt about Emilia was yielding its inevitable consequence in helpless hostility towards the injured one for pressuring him while he was still hoping to resolve the conflict between a son's duty and a lover's loyalty. As he would later insist, he had never denied their engagement and never told Emilia he would not marry her. What he had also not told her was that despite all the money coming in over the past four years, he had hardly anything in the bank to show for it. Extortionate commissions, travel, living and training expenses, legal fees and income tax, plus the remittances to his mother and the cost of the house he was having built in Sequals had swallowed up virtually all of his share of earnings from fights and exhibitions. His best, indeed, his only, hope of becoming the rich fellow most people thought him to be lay in winning the heavyweight crown. With that gracing his brow, no one – not even his mother – would deny him anything. But, for the present, how could the great and famous Primo Carnera, a hero to his people, ask anyone to believe that he was too poor to keep a wife on top of all his other expenses? Emilia should have had faith that he would eventually win his mother over to their side. Those nagging letters, that chasing after him from one capital to another, far from helping her cause was only turning him against her.

As for those two insignificant bouts set up in London, Carnera could not really blame Dickson or Sée. Britain produced very few top-rank heavyweights. There was vast potential, of course, among the Negro subjects of the Empire, but their prospects of being coached to win fame in any British sporting arena were almost non-existent. There was another reason why Britain could not come up with the brand of heavyweight fighters prevalent then – as now – in the United States. It was called 'clean fighting'. Generally speaking, you did not gouge, butt or rabbit-punch your opponent, however badly you needed that purse money. Winning was important, but so too was the respect of the fight fans and observance of the Queensberry rules, certainly as far as the referee was concerned. By the same token, matches between boxers of grossly unequal physical dimensions were in principle to be avoided. Back in 1929, the novelty value of 'Man Mountain' Carnera, coupled with his lack of experience and aggressiveness, had overridden most objections to the uneven matchings. Now, with three years and forty bouts behind the Italian giant, scruples were being voiced. On 27 March, four days after George Cook's fourth round defeat, again by a knockout, the *Sunday Express*, under the heading, CARNERA IS A MENACE, reminded its readers that it had protested, even back in 1929, against the exhibition of Carnera in circumstances 'more primitive than that of a Spanish bullfight. There were no suitable opponents for this ox of a man in 1929,' it added. 'There are [sic] none today.'

The writer, finding significance in the fact that Lord Lonsdale, noble patron of the noble art, had not been at the fight, had called him and been told, 'I did not attend the fight because I thought the matching was absurd. One was nine inches and five stone [seventy pounds] lighter than the other.' The writer then tilted back his fedora, loosened his tie and gave the story the full purple-tipped treatment:

> What happens at these exhibitions? You watch a giant fighting a fly. You see a man who is as terrifying in his physique as a Frankenstein monster. Carnera fights with the automatic precision of a robot. When an opponent lands a blow, his face is expressionless. Then his close-set dark eyes narrow and gleam strangely. The rubber gum shield clenched in his teeth is bared. The pale olive face becomes taut. He gazes down at his dwarf opponent. The effect is monstrous . . . Cook almost leaped from the boards to reach the Italian's face. The blow went home. Carnera did not wince. He was transformed into an animal. His great fist buried itself deep into Cook's ribs and it seemed the blow would disappear into Cook's body. He clouted Cook on the side of the head and sent him staggering sideways. He knocked Cook straight again . . . If Carnera had been a really great fighter, Cook would have been killed . . . That is the menace behind the use of Carnera and his dwarf opponents.

The writer was a gifted hyperbolist but a lousy tipster. 'The farce', he predicted, 'will be continued on 7 April when Donald McCorkindale, the South African champion, will be put into the ring against the human man-eater.' As for Larry Gains, the Canadian-born champion of the British Empire, who would be put into the ring with the monster robot the following month – he would be used as a 'chopping block'. In fact, McCorkindale went the full ten rounds with Carnera, to lose on points. And Larry Gains?

If proof were needed that Primo Carnera, despite his progress as a boxer, was not yet championship material, it was provided in the White City stadium on the night of 30 May. During the preceding two weeks, the Italian had flown back to the Continent and scored convincingly against the French heavy-weight champion, Maurice Griselle, and the German, Hans Schoenrath. But Sée and Dickson had come close to falling out over the match with Gains. The Frenchman had seen Max Schmeling knocked out in 1925 by Gains, the twenty-nine-year-old offspring of a Canadian Negro and his Italian wife. He had followed Gains's career since then, and his fear was not that the mulatto might come anywhere near to knocking out Carnera; what most concerned him was that with his greatly superior speed and technique he would make the younger man look clumsy and sluggish. And this at a time when Primo expected to be taken seriously as a contender for the title that was to be disputed between Sharkey and Schmeling in three weeks' time. Sée no longer had a percentage of Carnera's earnings, but he still cherished a hope that the Italian would eventually validate his Great Idea by winning the championship. Dickson, who thought this unlikely, was primarily concerned with setting up bouts that would draw the crowds, such as the 70,000 who flocked to the White City to see how the popular mulatto, 6 in. shorter and giving away about 68 lb, would shape up against the Man Mountain.

Gains was not exactly an ardent student of the works of George Bernard Shaw, but he obviously shared the Irish playwright's opinion that 'It's no good anyone trying to fight Carnera as if he were an ordinary man. He requires a special technique.' Whatever Shaw had in mind by 'special', Larry Gains's performance on the night must have exemplified it, and for just the third time in his career – the second, if we discount the 1930 Maloney 'robbery' – Carnera was defeated on points over the ten rounds.

It was a well-deserved win and it was no reflection on Gains's skills that his opponent totally failed, once again, to deploy the one weapon that might have decided the fight in his favour: a firmly closed fist, and his weight behind it. Shaw had dealt in the self-evident when he added, 'If Carnera had a right like

Dempsey's or Carpentier's . . . he could settle anyone.' The professional critic, Trevor Wignall, was more specific. 'Carnera', he wrote, 'is so anxious to indicate he is not a killer, he has grown into the habit of cuffing, with open glove. Until he discovers how to keep his glove closed, he will simply be another boxer.'

Another three and a half years would pass before the film star Cary Grant, a dedicated fan, could declare, 'Carnera is no longer a boxer but a vicious fighter.' Bill Duffy would be able to claim some credit for that. Sée, who had never pushed Carnera into punching his full weight, out of genuine fear for the consequences, would not even be around by then. The defeat by Sharkey, followed now by the Larry Gains victory, had perhaps shaken his faith in the theory behind his Great Idea. In sparing Carnera the early punishment and setbacks suffered by most novice fighters, had he not robbed him of the will and the need to 'get in there' in the spirit of the Manassa Mauler and never let up while the other guy was still standing?

At the same time, in that spring of 1932, Léon Sée must have been wondering, not for the first time, how a good bourgeois like himself, highly respected in his own country's sporting circles, could afford to remain involved with the New York branch of the Carnera management syndicate. Owney Madden, its dominant member, had been arrested in New York by detectives who had been searching for him since the State Board of Parole ordered his return to prison for violation of the terms under which he had been released from Sing Sing. In short, he had broken parole by reverting to his wicked racketeering ways. But to no one's surprise, he was released on bail a few days after his arrest and had again disappeared. He did not reappear until the summer, meanwhile bringing upon the judge who had set him free the censure of Governor Franklin D Roosevelt, who categorized his release, unless it was rescinded by an appeal from the Attorney-General, as tantamount to 'the destruction of the Parole Board'.

'Big Bill' Duffy had managed to keep out of jail, more by luck than merit, and was now pressuring Sée to make a complete break with Carnera, in Europe and in the United States. It was inconvenient, having the boxer still so dependent upon Sée. It irked when a newspaper quoted Carnera as saying, 'Sée is my mother and father to me. He takes care of me against crooks and whores in the United States.' It was getting time to have the big booby back in the States and under the syndicate's exclusive control. Walter Friedman would nursemaid him across the Atlantic. The fine levied by those clowns in Rome having been paid – and the money debited to Carnera's account, of course – the boxer could be put back to work again for the rest of the year. And Luigi Soresi would take over from Sée. He was Italian. He was a good front man: vice-president of the New York branch of the Banca Commerciale Italiana. What with that background and his command of the lingo, he was the ideal guy to explain to Primo how his earnings were being handled. Most important of all, you knew where you stood with Luigi – and he with you.

Everything was now converging towards the final break. There were exhibitions in England and Ireland during the weeks immediately following Carnera's defeat by Gains, but attendances were lower than usual. The boxer's own spirits were at rock-bottom. He had let down his French 'mother and father'. His own countrymen, writing in the Italian press, were deriding him. Emilia was ominously quiet and it was said she was talking to lawyers. Back in Paris, Carnera started to womanize and to drink heavily. 'Good time Charley' Friedman had arrived and was joining him in the fun, unlike M'sieur Sée, who could only complain and threaten to walk out on him if he didn't pull himself together.

Two years later, Léon Sée tried to put the best face on it when he wrote: 'Carnera did not really need me any more . . . so I let him return alone to the United States in June 1932. Important business kept me in Paris. I knew he was in good hands because I had entrusted him to a wise American manager, Bill Duffy, better situated than I was to overcome the final obstacle between Carnera and our goal: the match for the world championship.'

Maurice Eudeline, Primo's close friend and chief trainer from the boxer's first days at Saint-Germain-en-Laye, was the last of the original team to say *adieu* on the quayside at Le Havre. There were tears. There had to be a strong embrace but it could only work if the giant pugilist would lift the little Frenchman up off the ground, as he had done so often for the benefit of the press.

They looked towards the expectant bunch of photographers. Then back at each other. Eudeline shook his head slowly. Carnera nodded. They shook hands and Carnera turned and walked up the gangplank.

Léon Sée's excuse of 'important business in Paris' was, of course, as dishonest as his reference to 'a wise American manager' was cynical. What he had done, in plain terms, was throw Carnera to the wolves. There was logic, however shabby, in this. He had already sold for a fortune his stake in the boxer's American earnings to Duffy's 'syndicate'. He had kept his 17½ per cent interest in European earnings at the time when Journée had sold his equivalent share to Jeff Dickson; but the Italian giant's defeat by Larry Gains and subsequent breakdown of morale had seriously devalued his attraction to European promoters. Duffy might have agreed, on sufferance, to allow Sée to continue on the American management team, if only to please Primo; but it would be on an expenses-only basis, plus whatever Sée could fiddle out of the boxer's personal accounts. It was not an alluring option for a proud and educated Frenchman whose hopes of realizing the Great Idea had been weakened by Sharkey's victory in October 1931 and now, seven months later, dashed by Gains's. He was back in his beloved Paris with Rosie, their three sons, Paul, Alexander and Lucien, and their two daughters, Pauline and Quinny. He would return to full-time sports writing. Maurice Eudeline, who had lived with the Sées ever since he fell out with his own parents, could take care of the training camp at Saint-Germain-en-Laye. Sée himself would not be looking for another protégé with championship potential. He had lived that dream with Primo and had no wish to re-live it with a substitute.

He took up the pen again professionally and in 1934 he

published a paperback volume telling the story of the years with his Italian protégé, under the title of *Le Mystère Carnera*. There is no English-language version of the book and it appears to have had little, if any, circulation outside France. Yet it is a unique document, in which a famous prize-fighter's patron, mentor and business manager openly confesses, giving chapter and verse, how he and his gangster colleagues had, between them, 'fixed' for their client to win no fewer than thirty fights during their stewardship.* As already noted in Chapter 2, they were by no means the first to use this totally illegal practice. Sée's disclosures would neither have shocked nor surprised any of the sports insiders had they known about them at the time. But to the public at large and to the ordinary run of boxing fans, the revelations would have so discredited Carnera as to rob him of any further genuine *afición*. In fact, *Le Mystère Carnera* became, to the present author, more like a *Mystère Léon Sée* after he had talked to Sée's daughter Pauline, living in Paris under her married name of Pauline Gay.

She remembered that many of her father's friends in boxing and journalistic circles had tried to persuade him to abort the distribution of his book in France and to republish it without the revelations about the fixed fights. They were also anxious that Sée should refute the reports circulating at the time that it was his plundering of Carnera's earnings that had led to the break in their relationship. Pauline's father had ignored their advice and had gone unrepenting to his grave in 1963 at the age of eighty-three. She, her sister and her brothers had had to live with the stigma of the book ever since and were concerned not to 'open up all that stuff again'. They could throw no light on their father's motive in going public with his self-incriminating version of the Carnera story over the years 1928–31.

Of the conceivable explanations that tease the mind, the least persuasive would have been Sée's need for whatever money the book might bring in royalties. He was already rich, certainly a dollar millionaire in today's terms. The book had a limited sale

---

* Relevant data from Sée's book are reproduced in the Appendix.

in France but was not translated for publication in the United States or in Britain, where it might indeed have stirred some interest. It is possible, of course, that Sée's sole motive was ego-gratification: an urge to leave behind him a documented testament to his Svengali-like transformation of a fairground freak into a potential world champion. It still does not explain why he went to such pains to publicize the dirt about those fixed bouts in Europe and the USA; but there might be a clue in the fact that, according to Pauline Gay, Carnera remained estranged from the Sée family for several years following his return to the USA in the summer of 1932. She and her sister, both teenagers at the time, had been among 'Uncle Primo's' greatest fans. He had reciprocated their affection, taking time out to play games with them at their home in St Germain-en-Laye and during their year-long stay at Atlantic Beach, New Jersey. She has no doubt that 'those American gangsters' had managed to persuade the Italian boxer that the prime cause of his insolvency was Léon Sée's financial rapacity.

As an explanation of the estrangement, this has the ring of credibility about it and might account for the embittered Frenchman's decision to take a *je m'en fous* attitude towards the feelings of his former protégé. So far as his own reputation was concerned, Léon Sée tries to reduce any damage done by the book by representing his tactics as the inspired – and indispensable – formula for realizing the Great Idea: namely, the making of a champion out of a young and inexperienced boxer by protecting him from physical and psychological traumas during the early years as a prize-fighter. In Carnera's case, the formula was amply vindicated from 1928 to the summer of 1931, over which period, if we are to believe Sée, two-thirds of his opponents were paid to take a dive. From there on, a self-confident and physically undamaged Carnera could allow his arm to be raised in victory without a compulsion to lower his head.

7
Tragedy and Triumph!

Carnera arrived in New York aboard the Île de France in time to see Jack Sharkey take the world heavyweight title from Max Schmeling with a points win over fifteen rounds.

It was a disgraceful decision, with one of the two judges giving it to Sharkey, the other to Schmeling, and the referee, Gunboat Smith, exercising the deciding vote. The German, who had weighed in at 188 lb, had carried the fight to his 205 lb challenger almost from beginning to end, forcing Sharkey on the defensive round after round. At the end, in contrast to Sharkey's swollen face and closed left eye, there was not a punch mark on the champion. A storm of booing greeted the announcement of the winner and a majority of the experts at the ringside disagreed strongly with the verdict. Charles F. Mathison, whose vote as a judge had favoured Schmeling, had been a distinguished boxing critic for many years.

Outrageous though it certainly was, the decision was welcomed by Carnera's managers. A heavyweight title fight, whenever it might come, between two non-Americans such as Schmeling and Carnera, would make nobody rich. Their boxer had earned a return bout with the new American champion provided he could first win against one or another of such equal-ranking contenders as Stanley Poreda, Ernie Schaaf and Max Baer. Sharkey was rich but willing to become richer. He was 4 years older than Carnera and thought by many to be past his prime. He was also unlikely to put his title at risk for many months to come and would then choose from the ranking contenders an opponent he felt reasonably confident he could defeat, but who would be a 'drawing card' as far as the fight fans were concerned. Duffy had no illusions about Carnera's championship qualifications at this stage, but he was confident that after a year of carefully chosen bouts, under the expert direction of the new trainer, Billy Defoe, there would be more than a sporting chance that the Italian could take the crown from Sharkey. And the syndicate would see to it that in the meantime he would be more than earning his keep.

An already demoralized Carnera was now facing a programme of eighteen fights between 20 July and 30 December, in almost as many different cities of the United States, against opponents as varied in physique and skill as only that nation could provide. And, as Duffy put it to him bluntly, these fights, with only a couple of exceptions, would be straight bouts in which he could expect to get hurt, and badly, if he did not learn soon enough to block the other guy's punches and deliver his own with crispness and with some, at least, of the formidable power nature had lavished upon him. Primo respected Duffy for his prize-fight tactics, and it felt good to have a fellow-countryman like Luigi Soresi looking after his financial interests. But he missed the wise and avuncular presence of Léon Sée; and Billy Defoe, *simpatico* though he seemed to be, was no substitute for Maurice Eudeline – not as a friend, anyway. If he was to start on the last long lap to the title with a good heart, he needed to have one of his brothers by his side. Secondo was already working as a barman in London and seemed set to make a career for himself in the restaurant business. Severino, now just twenty, would jump at the chance of joining his famous elder brother in America. Bill Duffy raised no objection and the brothers became inseparable over the next two years.

The first three bouts, all staged in New York over a period of thirteen days, did Carnera's reputation no harm at all. Jack Gross was punched to a standstill by the seventh round; Jerry Pavelec was excused further involvement just fifty-one seconds after the start of the fifth round; a rugged Californian, Hans Birkie, was beaten on points over ten rounds. Paradoxically enough, the fourth bout, the only one Carnera lost that year, did more for his reputation than any of the others. His opponent, the Jersey City heavyweight Stanley Poreda, was clearly outboxed and outfought by Carnera for almost all of the ten rounds. In the opinion of James P. Dawson, the respected boxing correspondent of the *New York Times*, 'Carnera lost only the fifth and seventh rounds.' But at the end of the fight the referee, Joe Mangold of Atlantic City, raised Poreda's arm as victor, almost causing a riot among the 10,000 spectators and leading to Mangold's suspension, later, by the New Jersey boxing authority for 'an unpardonable decision'.

The circumstances of Poreda's 'win' advanced rather than retarded Carnera's steady progress towards a title fight with Sharkey. As Bill Duffy might have put it: 'With that bum of a referee as an enemy, who needs friends?' In Chicago on 9 December, a further boost for the Italian's credibility came with his second points victory over ten rounds against the formidable King Levinsky, whom he had defeated in the same city a year previously. Meanwhile, he had scored early-round knockouts against Jack Gagnon in New York, Ted Sandwina in Florida, Gene Stanton in Camden, New Jersey, Jack Taylor in Louisville and Len Kennedy in Boston. And there was a technical knockout at Madison Square Garden against the Portuguese giant José Santa, who was an inch taller than Carnera and only eighteen pounds lighter, and another against John Schwake in St Louis.

As in his 1930 and 1931 tours of the States, the human juggernaut from Sequals was carrying all before him, right up until the end of December, a month in which he took on no fewer than seven opponents, including Levinsky, in bouts which were sometimes only three days, but hundreds of miles, apart. The prize money kept rolling in and some of it even ended up in Carnera's own bank account. It did not stay there for long. Part of it was being remitted, piecemeal, to his cousin and former schoolmate, Francesco Carnera, who lived next door to

Primo's family and had a good head for business. The money was for the purchase of a site on the outskirts of Sequals and the building of a villa large and handsome enough to reflect Primo's future standing as Italy's first world heavyweight champion. There were also monthly remittances to his parents and his own out-of-pocket disbursements, usually measured less by the depth of his purse than by his generosity to everyone around him. As he assured the wide-eyed Severino, 'There's nothing to worry about, this is only spending money. Luigi, my banker, is looking after the rest.'

There had been no family reunion for Primo and Severino over Christmas of 1932, and there would be no break in training throughout January of the new year. Rivalries between top New York promoters, money considerations and squalid prize-fight politics were all combining to present Carnera with the possibility of a crack at the world title that very year of 1933.

The management of Madison Square Garden Corporation had over-stretched their finances by investing in the open-air Long Island Bowl designed especially for boxing, at a time when the heavyweight scene was devoid of any real crowd-pullers. In the meantime, the Garden had fallen out with the vastly influential Jack Dempsey and his syndicate, which now managed Max Schmeling, who was still being boycotted by the Garden's management. So the Garden made a deal with Jack Sharkey: he would defend his title some time in the summer, under the Garden's auspices, after two of the ranking contenders had fought an eliminating bout, under the same auspices, of course. Surprisingly, the chosen two turned out to be Primo Carnera and Ernie Schaaf. This was perhaps not so surprising, given that Sharkey happened to be a part owner of Schaaf's management contract and a close personal friend. He would obviously rather have his man share in what could be a useful purse from the Garden than present the takings on a plate to such other ranking contenders as Max Baer or Stanley Poreda.

The fact that both of them had beaten Schaaf was neither here nor there. Then again – perhaps it was. Schaaf was a clever enough fighter. If he could handle Carnera and win on points over the distance, he would then be matched against his pal Jack for the title, and this would suit Jack much more than having to take on Poreda or Baer. Those guys would want to win. After Ernie, Jack could rest on his laurels, if he chose to, for another year. And if Primo Carnera should screw things up by eliminating Ernie from contention? Sharkey had taken care of him once: he could do it again – and for a major share of the copious greenbacks New York's Italian community would shower upon the event. It was a sweetheart deal, totally bypassing the reality of the title contention, which should have recognized the prior right of Baer and Schmeling to an elimination bout. As it stood, these two would fight it out at the Yankee Stadium on 8 June, with the winner having to take on either Schaaf or Carnera. In turn, the winner of that bout would then wait upon Sharkey's convenience for a title fight.

On the face of it, the matching of Schaaf with Carnera on 10 February was fair enough. The former US Navy champion would be giving away 56 lb, but his *nom de guerre*, 'The Tiger of the Sea', had been well earned. He was in the first flight of heavyweight contenders and had been described as 'the most perfect figure of athletic manhood ever to enter the ring'. In his eight years as a professional, he had scored victories over Uzcudun, Stribling, Reggirello, Jack Gross and Baer, whom he had beaten on points over ten rounds in December 1930. Baer's revenge, two years later, with a brutal battering of Schaaf in Chicago, had more than evened this score, but the ex-sailor had had six months to recover before meeting his Italian co-contender.

The fight would be over fifteen rounds. Schaaf's chief second would be Jack Sharkey; Bill Duffy, Luigi Soresi and Billy Defoe would be in Carnera's corner. A special radio line would relay a live commentary on the fight to the bedside of the legendary Jim Corbett, first of the glove-wearing world champions, whose last fight – this one against heart disease – ended in defeat that very year. But the public at large, apart from the Italians, were not interested in the event, and with barely 19,000 spectators, Carnera's share of the purse would be only about £2,200. A local lawyer had secured a writ of attachment for £500 in respect of 'legal services', but writs of this kind against Carnera's purses were now commonplace.

There was more booing than cheering from the crowd as the fight progressed from one unexciting round to the next, with much clinching, some half-hearted attempts by both men to step up the pace, but too much wary sparring, interspersed occasionally with some good body-punching by Schaaf and some hard rights and lefts to the head from Carnera. By the end of the eleventh round, the Italian was ahead on points and Schaaf, having failed to break through his opponent's guard, had slowed down to a leaden-footed amble, with barely the energy to raise his arms. He rallied briefly in the twelfth round but was floored for a count in the thirteenth when a couple of right uppercuts were followed by a left to the jaw, seemingly with no great power behind it. Carried from the ring on a stretcher, Ernie Schaaf remained semi-comatose in hospital with inter-cranial haemorrhage and a partly paralysed left leg and arm.

During this time, Carnera, greatly agitated and unable to sleep properly, called the hospital almost hourly for news of his opponent's condition. Upon Schaaf's death, five days after the fight, the Italian was put under technical arrest on a charge of manslaughter and twice interrogated by the Homicide Squad while the post-mortem was being conducted. He remained devastated, even after being officially cleared of any responsibility for Schaaf's death. The autopsy revealed that the American had entered the ring with a blood clot on the brain, left over from the Baer fight. His death had resulted from an accumulation of blows rather than the thirteenth round knockout, and it seemed that the crucial damage had been done by Baer almost six months earlier, when he battered Schaaf senseless during the tenth round of their return fight.

Despite this finding, William Muldoon of the NYSAC promptly announced that Carnera would not only be barred from fighting Sharkey; he was too big to be taken on by any average heavyweight and in future would be allowed to fight only in a 'Dreadnought' class of pugilists, defined as weighing 240 lb or more and of a height not less than 6 ft 2 in. In effect, this would limit his opponents to just six contemporary professionals, four of whom, George Godfrey, Vittorio Campolo, José Santa and Jack Gross, he had already met and beaten, the last-named twice over. The remaining two were the giant Portuguese–American, Salvatore (Ray) Impellittiere, and Walter Cobb, neither of whom was of championship material.

The NYSAC bar would not have applied to a title fight promoted in a city beyond the commission's writ – an academic point since the champion, Sharkey, was under contract to Madison Square Garden, bed-fellow of the NYSAC. But since Sharkey and the Garden, in their wisdom, had decreed that either Schaaf or Carnera would compete for the title, and since Schmeling was barred by the Garden and Baer too dangerous an opponent, a way had to be found around the dilemma. No problem. The NYSAC simply restored Carnera to the status of Number One Contender and the Garden set 29 June as the date for the title fight. The Dreadnought ruling was suspended so far as championship bouts were concerned.

What Carnera wanted to do now was to get out of New York, out of the United States, away from the place where a good man's death was being attributed, directly or indirectly, to him and where morbidly fascinated crowds were lined up outside the cinemas for a look at the film showing the destruction of the Tiger of the Seas by the Man Mountain. Primo's mother, Giovanna, had telephoned from Italy, weeping as she pleaded for his reassurance that he had not killed a man in the ring, as people were saying. The call came before he had been exonerated. He was as anguished and bewildered as she was, knowing he had not even intended to go for a knockout blow, being already well ahead on points. There was little he could say to comfort his mother, but he told her he would be leaving for Sequals as soon as possible.

It would have been totally in character for Carnera to have

gone to Ernie Schaaf's mother as soon as her son's death was announced. In fact, what he did was write to her, pleading for forgiveness. In later years, his wife recalled how he treasured the mother's reply and often reread it. She had written: 'Don't blame yourself, my son. It was an accident and it was not your fault. It could have happened to you and then it would have been your own mother who would be crying, as I am now.'*

There would be many different versions of what happened between Carnera and Schaaf's mother. One account had it that there was a meeting in Boston where the mother, a German immigrant, was living and where the funeral took place. The two of them had embraced and cried together. A substantially different account is given in a book about Sequals written by Monsignor Giuseppe Dalla Pozza and published in 1982. After referring to the 1933 tragedy, the reverend author notes: 'Later on, Primo paid a visit to Ernie's aged mother, living in Germany, and unobtrusively left behind in an envelope the purse money he had received from the Schaaf fight.'

Not in doubt, and confirmed by those who were present, is that Primo, on arrival at Sequals, had a requiem mass offered up for the soul of the dead boxer. In spiritual terms, this would surely have been as welcome to the deceased as the Garden's purse money would have been to his old mother, wherever she was living at the time. Alas, effective support for either supposition remains stubbornly resistant to research.

It was during this visit to Sequals that Carnera was able to show off to his new European manager, Luigi Soresi, the villa he had paid to be built on the outskirts of the village. It was, and still is, an impressive two-storey residence lying back from the Via Roma, behind a formal front garden and driveway enclosed by tall and graceful outer walls and lofty iron gates. The same driveway gives access to a small one-storey building at the side of the main house. This, built and decorated in the same style as the villa, incorporates a garage and a large gymnasium,

* Santini, op. cit., p. 202.

equipped in the owner's days with everything a boxer in training would need, from parallel bars and punch bag to a full-size ring. Above the entrance to the gymnasium and running the width of the façade is the motto, MENS SANA IN CORPORE SANO in golden letters upon a light blue background panel, all worked in mosaic. It was a three-minute walk from the new house to the main square of Sequals, the Piazza Cesarina Pellarin. Another minute would take Carnera to his favourite bar, the Bottegon, on the Via Domenico Facchina. And a further few minutes' walk on down the same street would take him to his parents' home at Number 52, where he was born.

As the next challenger in line for the heavyweight crown, Carnera was, if not yet an Italian national hero, certainly a major celebrity and a source of patriotic pride to a people already being weaned from the sweet milk of *dolce far niente* to the raw meat of chauvinism and imperialist ambition. The boxer was later to be condemned by many for donning the black shirt of fascism on arriving in Rome after being fêted that winter and spring throughout the major cities of Italy. It was easy enough, with a few years of hindsight, to deride him for political opportunism or, at the least, naïvety. But to be an anti-fascist Italian in 1933 would have required – and did require – a far greater measure of political sophistication than could be expected of Carnera and of millions more of his fellow-countrymen. Mussolini's unprovoked invasion of Abyssinia (since renamed Ethiopia) was more than two years yet into the future. The Rome–Berlin Axis, binding fascist Italy to Nazi Germany, was even further ahead. In the meanwhile, the party created by *il Duce* when Carnera was thirteen had, by the time he was sixteen and working in France, won a parliamentary majority in a general election, crushed its socialist and communist enemies and secured the constitutional continuity of the monarchy. Five years later, it signed a treaty with the Pope, putting an end to the old quarrel between the Italian state and the church of Rome and recognizing the Vatican as an independent and sovereign state. All this would have been reason enough for an uneducated but patriotic Italian Catholic to be comfortable with *il Duce*'s leadership. There were others, infinitely better educated, throughout Europe and in America, who were more than just comfortable with *il Duce* at that time: they flattered and fawned upon him. In England, a brilliant politician named Sir Oswald Mosley had gone to the extent of forming a party that slavishly imitated everything about Mussolini's movement, even to the extent of copying its blackshirt uniform and its stiff right-arm 'Roman salute'.

The giant boxer would have cause enough for disillusionment with the fascists long before their pact of steel was forged with Hitler's Germany; but to be greeted in every city, that spring of 1933, by blackshirted *squadre* parading their banners and chanting the stirring refrain of *Giovinezza* was heady stuff for a 26-year-old political infant who had spent half his life in alien countries where Italians came under the heading of 'wops'. And to be invited on arrival in the Eternal City to meet the second most powerful person in the fascist party, Secretary Achille Starace, was understandably one of the highlights of his tour. Another was the announcement on 7 April that the Italian Federation of Boxing has conferred upon Primo Carnera the title of heavyweight boxing champion of Italy. In order to do this, the Federation had first deposed the reigning champion, Innocente Baiguera, on the grounds that he had been fighting in the United States without the permission of the Federation. This was a shabby excuse for taking the man's title away from him. In normal circumstances, a fine would have been considered punishment enough. The real reason was that Baiguera, as the Italian champion, ranked higher than Carnera in the Federation's books as the appropriate challenger that summer for Sharkey's world title. But there would be no US interest in such a bout. Therefore, 'The Italian king of the ring is dead; long live the new king.' And the new king, in accepting the honour, promised to do his utmost to bring to Italy its first world championship.

The tour was to end on 27 April with Carnera's departure for the United States on board the *Conte di Savoia* out of Genoa, where Luigi Soresi would be waiting for him. In the meantime, Rome was proving seductive. So were all the cities of the south, especially Naples, where he was presented to Crown Prince Umberto, heir to the Italian throne, and his wife, the former Princess Marie-José of Belgium, who let slip a wistful sigh after checking his 18½-in. biceps. Inevitably, he missed the ship at Genoa. A distraught Soresi chartered a seaplane with the object of catching up with the liner at Villefranche on the Côte d'Azur where, in response to Soresi's telegraph, the liner's captain had agreed to drop anchor and take them aboard. But the seas off Villefranche proved too boisterous for such an operation and the liner went on its way without Carnera, much to the agitation of the Madison Square Garden press agents, who were counting on the Italian colossus for the kind of arrival publicity that would help boost advance bookings for the big fight.

Carnera embarked on the liner *Rex* a week later and went straight into training during the Atlantic crossing. He had given the journalists at the quayside a broad hint that he had the best possible motive for winning the title from Jack Sharkey. Pressed to explain, he declared, 'I have been told by Achille Starace that if I win, it is a certainty that I shall be invited to meet *il Duce* in person.' There was perhaps another, and less exalted motive. While the boxer had been touring sunny Italy, a tragic tale had been unfolding for the edification of a press and public further north, in rainy old London town. Emilia Tersini, her patience all spent, had brought a breach-of-promise action against Primo at the High Court of Justice, King's Bench Division. Her case was presented by the eminent barrister and King's Counsel, Walter T. Monckton, who later served as a minister in several Conservative governments and was created a viscount in 1957.

At the time of the breach-of-promise action, he was serving as attorney-general to the Prince of Wales, whose closest confidant he became during the crisis leading to the Prince's abdication, as King Edward VIII in 1936. In the light of the Prince's personal interest in Carnera, already warmly expressed, it might have seemed injudicious for Emilia's solicitors to have engaged the Prince's best friend to conduct her case. But that would have been to call in question the moral excellence of the future king as well as his attorney-general. Such a slur – in the latter's case, at least – would have been totally unjustified, as the barrister proved with his brisk opening plea for the plaintiff. Monckton told the court that, according to the defendant, it had been agreed with Tersini that the marriage would not take place until his boxing career was finished. However, since he was not in court to support that contention, the only issues for the jury to decide were whether there had been a refusal to marry and, if so, what were the damages his client was entitled to recover.

After relating the circumstances in which his client and Carnera had first met, Monckton went on: 'Within a short time he was taken by the plaintiff to her home and introduced to her mother, and by October of 1929 he was a frequent and welcome visitor. In November, the parties agreed to marry, and the mother's consent was asked for and readily given. The defendant gave the plaintiff, first of all, a small signet ring which he afterwards replaced by one of greater value.'

With the jury in a state of spellbound anticipation, Monckton came to the matter of the letters written by the defendant. He was bound, he almost lamented, to read some of the private correspondence which passed between the parties to indicate the way in which the relationship began, their deep affection, and what each was prepared to sacrifice for the other. 'In letter after letter, the defendant professed in poetic language his deep concern for her, and there can be no doubt that they were very much in love with each other.' Before proceeding to carry out, with understandable reluctance, his distressing duty, counsel advised the jury that 'the letters, written in Italian, lost something in translation and might appear to be somewhat extravagant in language.' No, no! one can almost hear the jury cry, across the years – only to have their fortitude rewarded by such bathos as:

My Treasure, I have not forgotten you and will never forget you as long as my eyes remain open. My love, have patience yet awhile, as I shall soon be near you forever, in order not to leave you . . . When I come to Europe you will have whatever you want. You will have a beautiful little house and a fine motor car . . .

Warming to his theme of perfidy and betrayal, Monckton looked up from the documents and cried aloud, 'What sort of promises were those to make to a poor girl? She was waiting and trusting, yet the defendant, after offering her all those things, did eventually cast her aside as of little use.'

Carnera, who was not legally represented at the hearing, had admitted in a written statement to the court that he had indeed intended to marry Miss Tersini but – well, not quite yet. The judge summed up the case and the jury, after a short absence, returned a verdict for Emilia Tersini and awarded her £4,200 damages, the approximate equivalent in present-day purchasing power of £100,000.

Carnera had of course been badly advised in not defending the case at a time when he was in Europe and free to do so. And the amount of damages perhaps reflected, in part, the jury's disappointment over his failure to show up. Luigi Soresi, aware more than anyone of his boxer's financial straits, was alarmed into paying a flying visit to London in the hope of persuading Emilia to agree to some kind of deal over the damages. Not surprisingly, she went to earth, surfacing only after the frustrated Italian emissary was on his way back to Italy. The damages remained unpaid and, in Rome, Carnera tried to make the best of it by declaring that as soon as he could 'get some money together' he would go to London and reopen the breach-of-promise case. He then slipped into less heroic language by adding that in the meanwhile he would be giving Britain 'a wide berth'.

It would be a saintly loser of a breach-of-promise action who could be expected to find anything complimentary to say about his ex-fiancée, so perhaps Primo's cavalier comments about the case upon arrival in New York need to be judged in their distressing context. 'It was Emilia who proposed to me,' he told the *Sunday Mirror* before leaving for the Prompton Lakes training camp. And he went on to say (in his inadequate English, which the reporters customarily rendered in quotable terms): 'It isn't my fault if she fell in love with me. I think she liked me because I was hard to get . . . But now she has killed whatever thoughts I had of marrying by bringing this action. You can't have two fights at a time – one in the ring and one at home – and I prefer fighting in the ring, where your opponent is always in front of you.' Asked what he intended to do about the lawsuit Emilia was reportedly soon to bring against him for her money in the New York Superior Court, he declared he had had practically no free cash for the past two years and had borrowed heavily to build his villa in Sequals. The more authentic voice of the giant Italian was recorded a few days before he went into the ring against Sharkey.

'I no got dough. Everybody wants dough – dough – dough. I no got dough.'

Acting on Soresi's advice, he had just filed a voluntary petition for bankruptcy in the US District Court of New York. At this time, in addition to a judgment in favour of Emilia Tersini for $14,390, there were claims for $6,300 from Luigi Soresi for money lent, $125 from a Fifth Avenue tailor named Joseph Caliendo, $2,750 from lawyers for services rendered, $300 from the Hotel Victoria, where Carnera always stayed in New York, and claims (which he disputed), of $3,779 from Léon Sée and $1,250 from Jeff Dickson. Altogether, his liabilities totalled $59,829 against assets of $1,182, which included $560 in a Los Angeles bank, a motor car worth $300, a deposit of $65 in a Harlem bank and $50 worth of clothing.

The most pressing of all his creditors was Emilia Tersini, and with good cause, considering this debt would not be completely cleared until December 1937. In the meantime, all her lawyers could do was apply to the court for the sequestering of Carnera's purse money pending judgments as to the various creditors' claims. They succeeded in getting an injunction on the very day of the Sharkey fight, preventing Madison Square Garden from paying the Italian his $17,000 share of the gate. But they failed in successive attempts to have his earnings placed under a receivership. Soresi was always right in there, showing just cause why this should not be done. The purse from the Sharkey fight, for example, had already been assigned by Carnera to creditors, foremost among whom was Soresi himself. There was, he boasted, the '1,000-acre farm and 100-room villa' in Italy he had sold to the boxer. There was this house at Atlantic Beach, for which he had not yet been paid. All in all, Carnera owed him $99,000. The hearings would usually come up before a certain Justice Schmuck [*sic*] who was that only in name, not in nature. 'In all probability,' he pronounced, 'the farm is a figment of the imagination.' But since no satisfactory proof of this (the figment) had been produced, he would turn down, 'reluctantly', the request by Emilia's lawyers for a receivership. As the legal tussling over Carnera's purse money continued, the learned judge was afforded plenty of opportunities to come up with such perceptive homilies as: 'Except for one or two who succeeded in keeping what they won, prize-fighters are of such a low mentality they don't know money when they see it.'

That was hardly the case with Carnera, whose problem was that he never in fact got to see the money. From September 1928 to June 1932, his gross earnings, according to one contemporary source,★ had totalled £160,000 ($800,000). He could hardly have been stupid enough to believe that it had all been absorbed in expenses, commissions and taxes. He must have suspected that after more than four years of almost non-stop prize fights and exhibitions he should have more to show for it than a Chrysler Imperial, an ample wardrobe, a house in Sequals, an empty piggy-bank, worsening varicose veins and a clamour of creditors. Out of his sweat, Paul Journée, Léon Sée and Jeff Dickson had already made fortunes and were still claiming for 'unpaid loans'. If his current managers, Duffy, Soresi and the rest, were not also enriching themselves, they would have walked out on him without so much as a *buon giorno*. But now, with the world heavyweight championship at last within his grasp, he could actually contemplate an end to the mystery of those vanishing earnings. The big earnings for a victorious

★ Trevor Wignall, *Daily Express*, 12 June 1932.

contender in that pre-television era would come not so much from the purse money as from the fees he could command thereafter without even having to put the gloves on, except for some nice and easy exhibitions. Later, whenever he decided to defend his title – maybe once a year – the money at stake would surely be big enough to rule out any conjuring tricks by his managers.

His confidence grew with every new day of training under the one-time featherweight wizard Billy Defoe, who was teaching him more in one round of sparring than he had learned in ten rounds with anyone else, including dear little Maurice Eudeline. Bill Duffy was a daily visitor to the New Jersey training camp and there was always young Severino for company in the evenings. He was going to lick Jack Sharkey this time. The Boston Sailor had fought only once since winning the title and was now 31 years old. At 26, and with twenty-eight fights behind him since his defeat by the champ eighteen months earlier, Carnera had nothing to fear from someone who, let's face it, was one of the least impressive title-holders for many a year. And once the crown was his, he believed he could hold on to it for a few extremely lucrative years. There were no Dempseys or Tunneys dominating the heavyweight scene. Schmeling, who ought to win over the young and up-and-coming Max Baer on 8 June, had already shown he was afraid to meet Primo Carnera. In any case, a title fight between a 'wop' and a 'kraut' would make no dough for the promoters or the fighters. American national pride must be at stake. The first challenge would probably come from a ranking contender like Stanley Poreda, who had stolen a points verdict from Carnera a year before, with the connivance of the referee. As for Baer, the guy was such an irresponsible playboy and Don Juan, he would probably have faded from the contender ranks by the time Primo was ready to defend his title, some time in 1934. However, he was looking forward to attending the Schmeling *v* Baer fight at the Yankee Stadium, especially the bit when the master of ceremonies would summon him up into the ring to take a bow as 'the next challenger for the heavyweight boxing championship of the world – Primo Carnera!'

Max Baer defeated Max Schmeling by a technical knockout in the Yankee Stadium on 8 June 1933, before a capacity crowd of 60,000. This was a 15-round elimination bout for title contenders and one of the few occasions when Max Baer gave the clowning a rest and fought the way his friend and patron, Jack Dempsey, had always wanted him to fight, the way he had put down poor Frankie Campbell back in 1930. As if to show his disdain for the odds of 3 to 1 on the German to win, he came out full of fury from the first bell and kept slamming away at his opponent over the first eight rounds and fouling repeatedly, despite referee Arthur Donovan's warnings. But Schmeling, always the better tactician and himself no slouch in toe-to-toe exchanges, stayed clearly in command of the fight. Seconds before the bell sounded for the end of the ninth round, a lucky right hook so stunned the German that he made no effort to resist when Baer continued to slam blows at him after the gong had sounded. The Californian went for the kill in the next round, keeping up a lethal attack on the half-conscious German well past the moment when Arthur Donovan should have stopped the fight.

Three weeks later, before a less than capacity crowd at the Long Island Bowl, Primo Carnera challenged Jack Sharkey for the title of heavyweight boxing champion of the world.

Expert opinion as to his prospects had wavered right up until the night of the fight. Damon Runyon, writing in the *New York American*, had shirked making a prediction, playing it both ways with: '[Carnera] is not an instinctive fighter. He has no ferocity. But he has amazing speed for such a big man. When upwards of 250 lb is merely shoving a ham of a hand encased in leather against a human object, that object is apt to be damaged.'

The *New York Journal* went out on a limb with half of its front page taken up on the day of the fight by an artist's impression of a snarling giant crashing his fist against the chin of his crumbling opponent over a caption reading: 'A right hand

uppercut will shake loose the heavyweight crown and start this
monster on a reign of terror that will last for years.'

Mr Hype [*sic*] Igoe of the same newspaper (in Sharkey's
opinion 'the best boxing writer in the world') predicted a win for
his fan; but a colleague, W. S. Farnsworth, put his money on a
points win by the Italian over the fifteen rounds. Ed Frayne of
the *New York American* also predicted a Carnera victory, and
Max Baer went further than most by declaring that the
challenger would win inside the limit. 'Sharkey no longer has
the steam for so many rounds. He's had problems in training
and the guy's too unstable, up against a serious fella like
Carnera.'

George E. Phair fell back on verse in the *New York American* to
paint a colourful word-picture of an indeterminate outcome:

> Jack Sharkey was a sailor once,
> An able-bodied tar
> Who did a lot of climbing stunts
> On many a mast and spar.
> Tonight the noble gob will seek
> To climb a human mountain peak.
>
> Though Primo's feet are on the floor
> His dome is in the sky
> Where Alpine avalanches roar
> And blizzards whistle by.
> It takes a mighty mountaineer
> To knock an Alp upon its ear.

There was no such ambivalence among the thousands of Italo-
Americans who converged that night on Long Island Bowl from
every borough of New York City and from a hundred
Manhattan hotels and boarding-houses booked from every
Eastern city with a community of Carnera's fellow-countrymen.
It was estimated that there were 45,000 of them in the Bowl that
night to watch the first Italian ever in boxing history make a bid
for the heavyweight crown. 'And all over the world,' as Robert

Vattori put it, 'fifty million Italian hearts were palpitating and trembling for him.'

There had been a cable from Sequals: 'Primo, this evening we are praying for you. Mamma and Pappa.' And one from London: 'Despite everything, I hope you win. Emilia.' By a final count, ten out of thirteen boxing experts of the United States press were predicting a Sharkey victory; but as the hour of the fight grew closer, the bookmakers started to take their own counsel and by the time an aeroplane flew over the huge stadium trailing a banner reading, CARNERA – ITALIA the 6 to 5 odds on Sharkey to win had changed, making Carnera favourite by the same odds. Jack Dempsey had gone on record with, 'Carnera has made incredible progress in training. Sharkey had better be in top condition to go fifteen rounds with him. He's not wasting punches and he's hitting with precision, especially with his right, which was practically useless a couple of years back.'

The well-known vulnerability of Sharkey's nervous system had earned him such nicknames as 'The Weeping Warrior' and 'The Garrulous Gob'. But the same man who could never sleep on the eve of a fight, who could burst into tears over a referee's adverse ruling and shoot his mouth off in the middle of a slug-fest, had given the awesome Jack Dempsey, as he himself put it, 'living hell' for the first five rounds of their bout in 1927. What was now to be established was whether one of the most deadly punchers in heavyweight history could repeat his 1931 victory over the Italian while giving away 60 lb, or 4 lb more than he had in the first fight.

The titleholder was first in the ring, at 21.15 hours. Not the most popular of champions, he was nevertheless given the ovation his status merited. Two minutes later, when the giant challenger in his brilliant green satin robe climbed over the ropes and extended his arm in the 'Roman' salute, the Italo-Americans gave massive voice to their patriotic zeal, and kept it up until the bell sounded for 'Seconds out' and the referee, Arthur Donovan, barked the ritual, 'Shake hands now, then come out fighting.'

There were certain similarities between the battle that followed and the battle of 12 October 1931 at Ebbet's Field. Both men showed eagerness, when incited, to slug it out, toe-to-toe. And Jack Sharkey, whenever he could get past the Italian's guard, would punish him, as before, with hard hooks to the body. Otherwise, the fight ran a somewhat different course. Whereas Carnera in 1931 had made a slight gain in points over the early rounds with his long left jab, in this title bout it was the champion who made the going, so far as points were concerned, over the first three rounds. But this was a different Carnera from the Ambling Alp of Ebbet's Field. His greatly improved footwork was keeping him out of trouble from the ex-sailor's own dangerous left jabs, and he was using his great arms with skill and confidence to provide a hermetic defence, likened afterwards by Sharkey to 'the limbs of a tree you'd need an axe to cut through'. By the end of round three, despite his points lead, Sharkey was showing uneasiness at finding himself up against a much better fighter than he had expected to deal with that night. While his seconds worked swiftly over the seated champion during the interval, Carnera stood upright in his own corner, listening in silence to the obviously heartened Duffy and Defoe. Catching Severino's proud smile, he motioned him up to the apron of the ring and the two brothers embraced through the ropes, moments before the bell sounded for round four.

During this round and the one that followed, each fighter in turn stepped up his attack. But to Jack Dempsey, seated at the ringside, 'the agile Italian was already making his adversary look like a novice and Sharkey was obviously being thrown by this demonstration of power and agility'. Towards the end of the fifth, as champ and challenger slugged it out again, toe-to-toe, the fans, sensing an imminent and dramatic end to the bout, were on their feet, yelling for their favoured fighter.

Back in his corner, Carnera was told by Duffy that the title was almost his. What he had to do in the next round was 'Go out and get it.' The Italian nodded solemnly. At the opening of the sixth round, he missed Sharkey's chin with a right that struck his shoulder. In dodging a follow-up blow Sharkey slipped but was up at once. Carnera scored with a left jab; Sharkey replied with a weak right before being driven to the ropes, where he took a hard left jab to the stomach. Now on the defensive, the champion missed with a right to the challenger's jaw, but connected with the next one. Carnera kept after him and the end came with what the front page of the *New York Times* described next day as 'a terrific right-hand uppercut to the chin which almost decapitated Sharkey and brought Carnera the title'.

It seemed that, at last, the giant had punched his weight; and as the referee's count went on over Sharkey's inert, face-down body, Carnera watched in growing concern from a neutral corner. When 'ten and out' was reached, Arthur Donovan turned towards him to proclaim him victor. But it was only after the seconds had clambered into the ring and a dazed Sharkey was being helped to his corner that the anxiety on the Italian's face gave way to joy. He leaped and cavorted into the embraces of his seconds, his brother and everyone else clamouring to congratulate the first Italian heavyweight champion of the world. While the ring swirled with well-wishers and the Italo-American spectators went wild, a sour note was struck by Sharkey's manager, John Buckley, who called over the din for the victor's gloves to be examined, with the obvious implication that it had taken more than a set of bandaged knuckles to put the ex-champ out for the count. Carnera could only gape at Buckley in stupefaction until Duffy, having shouted to him to stay where he was, invited Bill Brown, a member of the NYSAC, to check the gloves.

There are many people, all deserving respect, who view professional prize-fighting with repugnance. Indeed, the mere fact that law-abiding adults will pay good money to watch a couple of strapping adversaries punch each other back and forth across a roped-off twenty-four-foot square of canvas-covered platform is beyond the comprehension of perhaps a large minority of the population of any civilized nation. It is an attitude that makes little concession to the fact that, in this century, boxers wear well-padded gloves and that prize-fighting is now governed by an accumulation of rules designed to reduce to a minimum the risk of serious injury, mental or physical, sustained in the ring. In terms of deaths per thousand events, prize-fighting is almost certainly less lethal than mountain climbing, motor racing, light plane flying and quite possibly septuagenarian fornication. As Joyce Carol Oates puts it in her stimulating book *On Boxing*:* 'Most of the time . . . death in the ring is extremely unlikely; a statistically rare possibility like your possible death tomorrow in an automobile accident or in next month's headlined airline disaster or in a freak accident involving a fall on the stairs or in the bathtub, a skull fracture, subarachnoid hemorrhage.' In precise terms, worldwide ring deaths, amateur and professional, rose from just one in 1918 to a maximum figure of 22 in 1953 before declining to 15 in 1964 and to 4 in 1984.†

But there are other sound reasons why opponents of professional pugilism will never succeed in having it banned. In no other sport do the rewards for excellence begin to match the money and prestige attached to the title of heavyweight boxing champion of the world. This gains particular point in the light of the fact that prize-fighting, more than any other professional sport, is the great leveller. As Dr Charles L. Larson, one-time president of the World Boxing Association, put it in his foreword to John D. McCullum's *The World Heavyweight Boxing Championship*: 'Wealth, education, inherited privilege and superficial cleverness are unimportant . . . Many of our most compelling champions rose from abject poverty, fought their first battles in such sordid surroundings as smoke-filled rooms . . . musty barns, in gambling houses . . . in a circus side-show, in the shadow of a tenement slum. Victory offers the only escape from such environments.'

In less than five years, a poorly educated and impoverished young Italian had made the journey from exile, hunger and

---

* Dolphin/Doubleday, 1987.
† *Ring Record Book & Encyclopedia*. Edited by Burt Randolph Sugar (Athenium, New York).

humiliation to the pinnacle of athletic achievement. He had earned purses totalling more than $300,000, the equivalent of around $2,850,000 in present-day terms. The crown was his. The title of 'champ' – unique accolade in a sport whose laurels are won by the individual deployment of strength, prowess and guts – that, too, was now his. But there was more to it, that June night of 1933, than the crown, the title, the laurels. These had been bestowed on ten other heavyweights over the forty years since Jim Corbett triumphed over John Sullivan in the first world title bout settled with gloves. During that time, scores of good fighters from Britain and continental Europe had crossed the Atlantic, thrown down their challenges and gone back home empty-handed. The title had in effect been monopolized by North America since 1889. Primo had done for his country what only one other European, Max Schmeling, had done for his: he had broken the monopoly. Like Caesar, he could declare, 'Veni, vidi, vici'. He had come, he had seen and he had conquered. And, like Caesar, he would now receive the acclaim of his fellow-countrymen.

It was unstinting. That night, and for days afterwards, New York belonged to Italy. The green, white and red *tricolore* was displayed from a thousand rooftops and tenement windows. Prominent in every shop window and restaurant, above every bar with the most tenuous of Italian associations, was a big smiling portait of Da Preem. Manhattan's Little Italy, that garlic-scented enclave south of Greenwich Village and north of Chinatown, gave itself over to a *festa* of music, song and impromptu parades.

The object of all this expatriate fervour, having dispatched an overnight cable to Sequals reading, 'I owe everything to you, Mamma', retired for half an hour or so to his suite at the Hotel Victoria with a pretty Italian girl from the Bronx before making an appearance at a party thrown for him by the Italo-American publisher Generoso Pope on the roof of the Hotel Delmonico at 59th Street and Park Avenue. From there, with the girl in tow, he and Severino joined their friends in a Brooklyn restaurant where the new champion drank a little too much wine for his pretty companion's liking, played an accordion rather badly and in his deep bass voice gave a rendering of 'O Sole Mio' as heartfelt as it was offkey. Meanwhile, Soresi was composing on Primo's behalf obsequious cables to Benito Mussolino and to the Secretary of the Fascist party, Achille Starace, in which the champion dedicated his victory to *il Duce* and to Italy. Mussolini's response, via his consul-general in New York, read: 'Express to Carnera my hearty congratulations and tell him that fascist Italy and its sport-loving people are proud that a blackshirt has become boxing champion of the world.' Starace's reply, direct to the champion, was another little gem of political backscratching.

'My prediction when I had the pleasure of receiving you in the Littorio Palace, has been fully realized. My warm approbation and my profound pleasure at a blackshirt having achieved such a brilliant victory.' No time was to be wasted in exploiting the propaganda value to the party of Italy's all-conquering modern gladiator.

Among the cables arriving at the Hotel Victoria next day was one from Emilia Tersini: 'Proud of your victory. I love you always'. There would surely have been a congratulatory cable from Léon Sée, but for whose obsession with the Great Idea a young Italian giant might have been left to work the fairgrounds of France; but there is no record of one. Press coverage on the morning after the fight paid generous tribute to 'Carnera's terrible left and almost hermetic defence' (*New York Times*) and proclaimed him 'the most formidable pugilist in the history of boxing' (*New York American*).

The Herald Tribune was almost lyrical in its praise: 'Carnera has proved to be Primo in fact as well as in name. The tremendous right uppercut, brought up with incredible destructive power from those famous and enormous feet, crashed like an express train on Sharkey's chin . . . Carnera, who has managed miraculous progress, now seems like an immovable rock, a bulwark against which all attempts by opponents can only be miserably shattered. Only dynamite could compete with this strength. But a dynamite that can be put to use in the ring has yet to be found.' The *New York American* further declared that 'Primo Carnera, regarded up to yesterday as a joke of nature or, at the best, a fairground booth attraction, has become world champion thanks to a right uppercut in which there seemed to be concentrated the strength of all forty-three million Italians. This precise, crisp and deadly punch laid Sharkey out cold on the canvas.' And the *New York Journal* went out on a limb with: 'He will become one of the most popular sovereigns of the ring in the annals of boxing.'

Such predictions must have brought a little comfort to Carnera when the spoils of his victories were laid out by his managers. The gate receipts for this poorly attended title fight totalled £32,000, out of which Sharkey, on 42½ per cent as champion, received £14,000 and Carnera, on 10 per cent as challenger, got £3,200. That was what he earned. What he put in his pocket after commissions and expenses was £90.

This, rather than the violence in the ring or the clamour of the fans, was and is the real ugly face of prize-fighting.

Towards dawn, as Severino and his big brother made their sleepy and happy way back to the Hotel Victoria, Primo, speaking Friulano, asked what Severino would like from him as a memento of that great night. 'Just one thing,' the younger brother replied, without hesitation. 'The glove you were wearing on your right hand when you knocked out Jack Sharkey.'

Severino died in 1964, a citizen of the United States. His widow Mary, whom he married in 1941, lives in Nutley, New Jersey. Today, more than half a century after it was used to such devastating effect, the glove remains in her safe keeping.

8
Hollywood's Fatal Lure

Television in the home was still an unrealized dream back in 1933. There had been plenty of still photographs of Carnera in the press, some cinema newsreel coverage and occasional radio interviews. But there was now an intense public interest in seeing the new world champion close-up and in the flesh. It was an interest that, short of having a seat at or close to the ringside during one of his fights, could best be satisfied by paying to watch the giant's appearance in exhibitions. Offers from would-be promoters of these came flooding in and were assessed with beady-eyed avarice by the Italian's managers. For Duffy, Madden, Soresi, Friedman and the rest, this was what it had always been about, from the time they had lured the young Italian to the States. The build-up of fights had produced chicken feed compared with what they could now reap from the mystique of the world championship, and there were three summer months left to put the holder of the sporting world's most prestigious title to work before he was committed to leave for Rome to honour a promise made to Starace.

For a fee of $4,500, Carnera appeared in Atlantic City on 2, 3 and 4 July, sparring three rounds a night with a kangaroo trained to go through the motions of boxing. Even to such a good-natured fellow as Primo, it must have been a hard act for him, appearing to share the spectators' hilarity as he parried and blocked the kangaroo's gloved paws. Certainly it would have been a relief after that to act out his exhibition routine on the stage of a Manhattan theatre over a fourteen-day engagement for which his managers received $20,000. The money rolled in as he toured the States during the next two months, travelling first class, sleeping in luxury hotels, eating *à sa faim* but 'protected', as always, from having to peruse boring statements from accountants and bank managers. That was Soresi's job, and Soresi, like Brutus of old, was an honourable man . . .

That summer, while Carnera was on tour, the front office at the Metro-Goldwyn-Mayer studio in Hollywood was casting actors for yet another movie about a promising young boxer who, having made it as far as a title bout, puts everything in jeopardy for a beautiful woman. It was to be an important production, with Otto Kruger already cast as the boxer's manager, John Huston's father, Walter, and Myrna Loy in key roles and Jack Dempsey playing a referee. Max Baer had been tested for the part of the boxer and immediately signed up on the strength of his dimples, dark curly hair and Pepsodent smile. His physique was no drawback, either.

The title of the film was to be 'The Prizefighter and the Lady' for American and world exhibition, but for Britain it would be retitled 'Everywoman's Man', for whatever obscure reason. The movie was still only in preparation when Carnera won the title from Sharkey. After that, it was only a question of how soon some bright spark at MGM would come up with the idea of casting the Italian champion as Baer's opponent in the climactic scene where the dimpled hero redeems himself with his fans and with the object of his affections by slugging it out with a Neanderthal. (So whoever claimed that Sylvester Stallone was a creative genius?) The bosses at MGM jumped at the idea. Carnera was already filling theatres and exhibition halls across the States. In real life, he would almost certainly have to defend his title against Baer while the movie was still on general release. And to cap it all – 'But for Pete's sake, guys, don't labour this before he's finished shooting' – that ugly great wop couldn't make a more perfect foil for our Californian Golden Boy'.

The immediate response by Carnera's managers to the MGM

offer should have been a firm and unshakeable, No. There was probably little reason at the time to fear that the playboy Maxie would take the title from the greatly improved fighter Carnera had become. But why upgrade the contender's chances by allowing him to rehearse his moves and test the champion's reflexes over take after take in a Hollywood studio? Instead of rejecting the offer out of hand, Duffy and Soresi involved themselves in an absurd dispute about the script. This called for Baer to win the fictitious fight. 'No way!' Carnera's managers declared. There was too much pride at stake. Their boy was the world champion. The script would have to be changed to take that into account.

The bargaining went back and forth, with Duffy and Soresi giving more and more ground as the MGM negotiators raised their offer, for what would be only a few days' work before the cameras, from $15,000 to $20,000 and finally to $25,000, at which figure the deal was clinched. The revised script would call for Max to win the first round, Carnera the next seven, and then for the hero, spurred on by his woman, to win the last two rounds with an appropriate display of all-American guts and valour. The fight, refereed by Dempsey, would be declared a draw, thereby cushioning the Italian's pride while leaving open the possibility of a fictional rematch should the movie do well at the box-office.

In fact, the fight scenes turned out to be far and away the most exciting ever shot, up until then, for a feature film. Put out on release before the real-life title fight of June 1934, the movie packed the cinemas everywhere – even for a while in Germany, until the Nazi censors suddenly realized that the curly-haired hero was not only of Jewish descent but was the boxer who had KO-ed the former heavyweight champion, Max Schmeling, in 1933.

Max Baer's fee from MGM was substantially lower than Carnera's; but in a very special sense, what he lost on the roundabouts he more than gained on the swings. In the course of the fictional fight for the cameras – the equivalent of about thirty rounds – he learned that the Italian was wide open to overhand right swings, brought up from the floor. This, not the studio's fee, was the best pay-off Max Baer would ever get in his life.

On 30 September, Carnera and Soresi arrived at New York's Pier 90 ready to embark for Italy aboard the splendid luxury liner, the *Conte di Savoia*, where the boxer was always treated as a VIP, with facilities for training during the voyage and a specially constructed bed measuring 7 ft 8 in installed in his stateroom. They arrived, but they did not embark . . . Once again they had missed the boat, which was now heading towards the Atlantic with Severino, two hired sparring partners and all the baggage on board. This time, they were able to catch up, courtesy of a steamboat and the *Conte* captain's indulgence, and give the passengers, once again, no excuse for not knowing who that giant was, tucking into a mountain of pasta at the captain's table every night.

The time had come for the new world champion to fulfil the promise he had made to Starace and to receive the honours that were to be showered upon him by a proud and grateful nation. He was already a celebrity with the ordinary run of his fellow-countrymen. He was viewed with opportunistic interest by the shrewd and calculating Secretary of the party. But it has to be noted that, to their shame, it took nothing less than the victory of 29 June to switch the Italian press and the sporting circles of Rome from an attitude of cold disdain towards the boxer to one of obsequious hero-worship. Roberto Vattori, writing many years later,[*] pulled no punches in recalling this craven *volte face*:

Up until the eve of his title win, the Italian fascists and press had paid little attention to Primo Carnera except to sneer at him, seemingly out of irritation from letting the giant slip out of their hands. He was a remote object, almost a foreigner, of very little interest and no particular value. To the Roman press he was some kind of Friulano who had happened to

[*] Op. cit., p. 103. Author's translation from the Italian.

become a boxer, from some unknown village up there near the Yugoslav frontier. It took the title win for the press to fall over itself with enthusiasm and for the fascists to hail him as the symbol of Italian virility. Now, the whole nation was made aware that the champion was a son of Sequals, a Friuli village close to the River Piave . . . The commander of the 55th Alpine Legion of Gemona made him an honorary Blackshirt corporal. He was entered in the Mille Miglia car race as partner to the famous Nuvolari, but the car broke down under his weight. And still the press couldn't give him enough coverage. The hide of a bison had to be used to make his gloves. With one punch he could kill a bull or crack a palace's pillars. He was a walking mountain, a whole street stood up on end. The fascist press used the Friulano for its own purposes. But he owed nothing to fascism. On the contrary, fascism owed a great deal to Primo . . . Fascism sought to represent him as a pure and typical model of the Italian at his best. But as a boxer, he was a creation of France and his career was carved out in the USA.

Carnera might have owed nothing to fascist Italy but Italy, nevertheless, was his motherland. The crowds that greeted him so tumultuously when he disembarked at Genoa were his fellow-countrymen. The Friuli villagers who carpeted with flowers the last miles of his journey and the men of Sequals who bore him on their shoulders from the motorcade to the embrace of his mother, these were his people, addressing him in the language of his childhood,

> *Tu sòs partît canai*
> *par 'zî lontan a fâ furtuna**

a language that sprang more readily to his lips than his almost adequate French, barely adequate English and inelegantly spoken Italian.

Politics was something totally beyond his comprehension or

---

* 'You left as a child, to seek your fortune in distant lands.'

interest. If Italy was happy to be governed by Benito Mussolini – and it seemed to be – that was fine with him. If the party and the press were now eager to pay their respects, what could be more flattering to an exile on one of his rare homecomings?

How about this tribute in the fascist party orders of the day, to someone who had not yet been called upon to serve even twenty-four hours in the militia:

> Blackshirt Primo Carnera of the 55th Friulano Alpine Legion, in winning the heavyweight boxing championship of the world for fascist Italy, has proved his exceptional physical and moral gifts and demonstrated the tenacity and will to victory of the blackshirts.

And the comment that followed in the *Gazzetta della Sport*, the same journal that had predicted, after the Islas bout in Milan, back in 1928, that he would finish up either back in the fairground or in a carpenter's shop:

> With this tribute, the first Italian boxer ever to become a world champion receives one of the greatest honours to which a soldier of fascism can aspire: a solemn eulogy by the General Commander of the Militia, holding him up as an example of the tenacity and will to win that typifies the new Italian.

So let bygones be bygones. It was his country, right or wrong. He had come back to redeem a promise. His first defence of the title would be in Rome and it would also be the first time the title had been put on the line outside the Americas since 1914, when the then champion, Jack Johnson, defended it successfully against Frank Moran in Paris over twenty rounds. But Johnson was then in exile from his own country, dodging a jail sentence for violation of the Mann Act. By contrast, Primo was the homecoming hero bearing, like Julius Caesar, the gift of a glorious victory won in a distant land, the gift now acknowledged by a hymn written in his honour by Monsignore

Emilio Carrara, to be sung by the choir of the Sequals parish
church:

> From the hills encircling our fertile plain
> Echoes your people's proud refrain,
> Telling how they rejoice in you,
> In your mighty arm and your heart so true.
> This is our hymn to a valiant son,
> To his glory abroad, to his victories won.
> Primo Carnera, flower of our seed,
> First in name and first in deed.*

And there was the other gift he brought with him: the entire
purse money that would be due to him from the forthcoming
fight in Rome. It would go to fascist party sport funds, as he had
promised the president of the Italian Boxing Federation. He
would be defending his title over a distance of fiteen rounds
against the European heavyweight champion Paolino Uzcudun,
the same 'Bull of the Pyrenees' whose woodcutter punches had
left him racked with pain for days after those gruelling ten
rounds in Barcelona back in 1930. As the *Guinness Book of
Records* put it in later years, between them they would constitute
'the greatest tonnage' ever in a world title ring, with Carnera
weighing in at $259\frac{1}{2}$ lb and Uzcudun at $229\frac{1}{4}$. But – Uzcudun as
first challenger to the title? Circumstances had led to it. The two
top-ranking contenders, in terms both of credibility and money
at the gate, were now Max Schmeling and Max Baer. But they
were both under contract to Jack Dempsey, who was currently
at war with Madison Square Garden, who owned the right to
promote Carnera's first title defence. Young Stribling was eager
to challenge and Jack Sharkey was entitled, in principle, to a
return bout some time, but no one could see much profit in
either of these potentials, least of all Dempsey. Stribling was not
much of a draw any longer. The gate for the Sharkey *v.* Carnera
fight had totalled only $120,000, against the $300,000 Dempsey

---

* A free translation from the Italian, by the present author.

was confidently expecting from a return bout between Baer and Schmeling in San Francisco later that year.

Finally, and not to be ignored now that he was king of the ring, was Carnera's pledge to stage at least one defence of his title in Rome against the only credible European contender, Paolini Uzcudun. In normal circumstances, the Garden bosses would never have countenanced a first title defence outside the USA; but, *faut de mieux*, and for a consideration, they decided to make an exception. Paolino was no pushover, but Primo should be able to handle him again, fighting in his own native country with properly fitting gloves and his new-found punching power. In return for the Garden's blessing, the champ's next two fights would be in the States and under the Garden's aegis.

Installed now in his fine new villa at Sequals and training seriously for his date in Rome on 22 October, Carnera felt happier than he had in years. Up at dawn, then a few miles of roadwork with one or other of his sparring partners over well-remembered terrain against a backdrop of the seven hills that had given the village its name (a Friulano corruption of the Italian, *sette colli*). Breakfast with Mamma, who had moved into the 10-room house with Sante, Severino and Secondo, who had taken leave from his job in London to bask in his big brother's reflected glory. Then a full day's work in the gymnasium under the direction of Billy Defoe, while Luigi Soresi laboured at the village post office over telegraphic connections with Rome and New York. There would be a succession of short breaks from gym work for the benefit of photographers and reporters from all the principal cities of Italy and Europe.

After the evening meal came the best hour or so of the day for Primo, making the rounds of the village with his father and brothers and his old school friend and cousin, Francesco Carnera, known to everyone as Checu (pronounced kay-koo). Two years younger than Primo and the 'brains' of the extended family, Checu had overseen the building of the new house from start to finish. He had already started to assemble a collection of photographs and press cuttings relating to his cousin. It was a labour of love that continued until Primo's death and is displayed proudly to this day for anyone, such as the present author, with a genuine interest in the subject. He still lives in the house next door to the one where Primo was born, on the Via Gian Domenico Facchina, and where Secondo's widow, Marianna, lives between occasional trips to London to stay with the families of her sons, Elvio and John.

Speaking in Friulano, through an interpreter, Checu recalls how he asked Primo on the eve of his departure for Rome in October 1933 if he believed he might be the first boxer to defeat the powerfully built Basque by a knockout. Carnera doubted it, but not because he considered Uzcudun invulnerable to a blow on the point of the chin with the champion's full weight behind it. It was a question of the Basque's height. Despite his weight, he was not quite 6 ft tall and he fought most of the time in a crouch. Carnera fought upright, his best stance for scoring with straight left jabs. A right-hand cross or swing would probably only part the air over Uzcudun's head. To deliver an uppercut, Carnera would have to bend his knees and expose his own head to a counter-punch. Of course there was always the possibility of luck, with his opponent's guard down at the precise split second he, Carnera, was positioned to deliver. And these days he was fast enough and confident enough to make the best of such an opportunity.

But Lady Luck was to prove as elusive as ever . . .

The champion arrived in Rome by air from Udine, the nearest airfield to Sequals, together with his father, his brother Severino, Luigi Soresi and Billy Defoe. When he appeared on the balcony of the Plaza Hotel to greet the crowds choking the Via del Corso he was wearing the uniform of the fascist militia. According to his cousin Francesco, it was Soresi who talked him into flaunting the black shirt on this occasion and again when he slipped off his dressing gown in the ring on the night of the fight. Whatever the truth of it, the gesture went virtually unreported in the Western democracies, where Italian fascism was regarded as a rather comic political aberration until the invasion of Abyssinia in September 1935.

It had been decided that the most suitable arena for the fight would be the Piazza di Siena, an open area normally used for equestrian events in the Villa Borghese gardens, less than a mile from the city's main railway terminal. Any other venue for the fight would have presented the police with an insuperable problem of crowd and traffic control. The piazza was transformed into an amphitheatre seating 55,000 spectators, almost half of whom turned out to be women. Carnera's two sparring partners, Harold Mays of Bayonne, New York State, and Arthur Huttick of New York, had been matched in preliminary bouts againt an Argentinian heavyweight and one of Uzcudun's Spanish sparring partners. Mays took care of the Argentinian with just two punches in their first round and Huttick won the decision after four rounds with the Spaniard. At the tail end of the preliminaries and ten minutes before the big fight began, Benito Mussolini arrived at the piazza together with his sons Bruno and Vittorio, his son-in-law Count Ciano and the Secretary of the fascist party, Achille Starace. After being escorted to a regal box upholstered in red plush and situated fifty yards from the ring, Mussolini responded to the routine roar of 'Duce! Duce!' with the Roman salute and the out-thrust bullfrog chin. Then he and his sons no doubt turned to prognostications about the fight; not the outcome, which could never be in doubt, but the round in which Carnera would unleash the uppercut that would lay out Uzcudun, second time champion of Europe, for the first time in his pugilistic career.

On entering the ring, Carnera also responded with the Roman salute to the crowd's ovation, after removing his dressing gown to reveal the black shirt that had been specially tailored for his bulk. A few minutes later, battle was joined.

As a championship fight, it could go to fifteen rounds. And it did, to the chagrin of those of the paying customers who, while not wanting it to end too soon, were counting confidently upon the drama of another knockout win by the national hero, this time smack in the heart of Rome, site of the gladiatorial games of yore.

There was no questioning the fairness of the verdict: a

Carnera victory by points over the distance. This was a totally different Carnera from the pugilist that Uzcudun had pounded so severely during their first bout, in Barcelona. He was cool and workmanlike, preserving his defence with agile footwork and good forearm blocking, and using that stabbing left glove to open cuts in the Basque's face within the first two rounds. By the end of the fifth round, Uzcudun was bleeding from his forehead, cheek and mouth. But he continued to slip Carnera's right uppercuts during the next few rounds and occasionally summoned the guts and energy to slug it out, toe-to-toe, with the champion.

By now the spectators, while marvelling at the speed and skill their giant was showing in the ring, were beginning to wonder how much longer he intended to play with his clearly outclassed opponent. In particular, they could not understand why, from the ninth round onwards, Carnera was using his right arm purely in defence while keeping up the point-scoring only with the left glove. There was a simple, almost banal, explanation. His right hand had come off worse from an impact with Uzcudun's thick skull and was completely out of action except as a blocking instrument during the rest of the fight. It was a bad sprain, with the knuckle bones badly bruised and one almost fractured. The film of the fight showed the champion using his left hand exclusively after the ninth round, and the doctor who examined the right hand afterwards advised two months' rest before he used it again in the ring.

There were bitter complaints by the Romans that their idol had not given them their money's worth by knocking the Basque out long before he damaged his fist. Nevertheless, he had come out of the fight with two more titles added to the big one: heavyweight champion of Europe and undisputed champion of Italy. And the next morning – honour of all honours – he was received in audience by *il Duce* at the Palazzo Venezia where, for half an hour, the fascist dictator questioned him about his experiences in the United States and his plans for the future.

While his right hand was healing, Carnera made a series of

public appearances throughout Italy, accompanied by Soresi
and Severino. He had promised his parents he would spend
Christmas in Sequals before returning to the States to train for his
second title defence, which would be against Tommy Loughran
in Miami on 1 March. He kept the promise, but it was a close
call. Now that he was champion, the lawyers acting in New York
for Emilia Tersini were stepping up their pressure for the
recovery of her breach of promise damages. They were still
trying to have his purse money put into receivership, but the
whole question revolved around the issue of jurisdiction: had an
American court the power to enforce the judgment, in a civil
action, of a foreign court against a legal resident of the United
States? The good Judge Schmuck, as we have seen, was treading
water over this. In the meantime, Carnera was in danger of
losing his status as a resident of New York if he failed to set foot
in the United States before the end of the year. On 16 December
the New York press reported, without going into the reasons,
that 'Primo Carnera established some sort of record by arriving
in this country on Wednesday and leaving for Italy on the *Conte
di Savoia* two days later.'

The main reason for maintaining residential status was to
frustrate as far as possible the British court's judgment in favour
of Emilia. As world champion, Carnera would otherwise have
been free to come and go as often as he pleased. And it begs the
question: why waste the time and money on a luxury liner trip
from Genoa to New York and back again instead of paying off
some, at least, of the debt to the former fiancée? Part of the
answer might have lain in the bitterness Carnera felt towards
Emilia for all the harassment she was giving him. But, in any
case, the voyage, with all its trimmings of staterooms for the
champion and his manager, first-class dining and win-
ing and training facilities, were 'on-the-house'. A full-size
boxing ring was set up every day in one of the vast and magnificent
salons of the *Conte di Savoia*, where Carnera fought a few rounds
with a sparring partner for the benefit of the passengers
seated at ringside tables with white-coated stewards lining
the walls behind them. So . . . on with the show, and eat your

heart out, Emilia Tersini.

There had been absolutely no excuse, other than the greed of his managers, to put Carnera into the ring with any of the contenders so soon after he had won the heavyweight crown. A new world champion need defend his title only about once a year, and then only if the money looks good. Betweenwhiles, he would capitalize on his unique status in every way other than by exposing it to risk in the ring. In the case of the Loughran challenge, Carnera, on the face of it, had everything to lose and little to gain. He would be confronting a former light heavyweight world champion, now fighting as a heavyweight but nevertheless giving away almost 80 lb. To most people, a win by the champion would hardly enhance his image. To the *conoscenti*, on the other hand, the Italian was in danger of losing his title on a points decision unless he could knock out Loughran early in the fight. And there were real doubts about this. The 31-year-old Philadelphian would be the fastest opponent, both in defence and attack, Carnera had ever met. He had beaten Max Baer and Jack Sharkey and made rings around such fighters as Campolo, Risko, Schaaf, Levinsky, and even the ace stylist Georges Carpentier. He had defeated James J. Braddock, who was to win the world championship in 1935.

But the bookmakers, in favouring the Italian title-holder, were showing they believed Loughran's best days were now behind him. And so they probably were, which is why Bill Duffy agreed to put him against Carnera. As Tommy explained it later, it was also a case of the Irish looking after their own. His friend, Father O'Leary, went to Bill Duffy and reminded the gangster that he owed the priest a favour for some reason or other (perhaps for dispensing a relatively light penance and absolution after hearing one of Duffy's more chilling confessions?) The favour he asked was a chance for Tommy to fight the champ. At first, Duffy declined on the grounds that he did not want his man made to look stupid by the clever Philadelphian. Father O'Leary persisted, perhaps even throwing in some free 'indulgences' to shorten Duffy's stretch in purgatory. Finally, Duffy agreed.

As Tommy saw it, his biggest problem on the night would be to prevent the massive Italian's weight from wearing him down in the clinches. His manager came up with an answer to that.

After we weighed in he went out and he bought a jar of the most sickeningly sweet-smelling hair grease he could get. After we got our instructions in the center of the ring and went back to the corner, he had taken this stuff out and he put a big slab of it on the crown of my head. As soon as we'd go into a clinch, I'd put my head right up under Carnera's nose, and I still have pictures of Carnera, in sheer disgust, trying to shove me off.

Well, maybe . . . But Loughran would have needed something more powerful than hair grease to avoid defeat in Miami on the night of 1 March 1934. By sheer skill and agility he managed, as expected, to make the champion appear to be more awkward and ponderous than in fact he was by this stage in his career; he even got the better of him on points in rounds three, four and six. From there on, irritated rather than hurt by Loughran's stinging combinations, Carnera went on the attack with his left jabs and kept them up until the end of the fifteenth and last round. He hadn't the speed or the skill to nail his plucky opponent with a knockout punch, but there was very little fight left in Loughran when the final bell sounded. He had waged one of the best fights of his fifteen-year career, with a challenge that, unfortunately, drew the smallest gate ever taken for a heavyweight title bout. Loughran's 12½ per cent of the net earned him $5,000. Carnera's 37½ per cent yielded $15,000.

It had been Carnera's eighty-third professional fight in less than six years, and roughly half of the bouts had been against American heavyweights, of whom only a minority had accepted money to take a dive during the early years of the Man Mountain build-up. His first-ever American opponent, Young Stribling, had helped him along the way – while lining his own pocket – with the staged bouts in London and Paris. Such was the play of destiny that, less than four years later, that raw young boxer of 1929 now wore the heavyweight crown, with Stribling just one of several aspirants to the throne. What would have happened had he and Carnera faced each other again in the ring, in honest combat, must remain conjectural. On 3 October, Young Stribling died after a road accident while he was on his way to visit his wife and their new-born child in hospital.

A few days after the Loughran bout, Carnera drove his Chrysler Imperial to Macon, Georgia, to a memorial service for 'Pa' Stribling's son. While in the locality, the champion accepted an invitation from the governor of the federal penitentiary at Atlanta to give an exhibition for the inmates before returning to New York. By all accounts, the arrival of the giant Italian in that grim penitentiary produced more of a *frisson* among the inmates than any bevy of Broadway showgirls would have sparked. One prisoner in particular was so excited that he dashed from window to window so as to keep Carnera in sight as long as possible. But then, as already noted, Al Capone – yet to be moved to Alcatraz – had long been an ardent fan of the noble art of boxing, when not preoccupied with other forms of combat.

In the opinion of James J. Johnston, vice-president in charge of boxing for Madison Square Garden, the three most eligible contenders now for Carnera's crown were Max Baer, Steve Hamas and the winner of a bout between King Levinsky and Walter Neusel, set for 8 March. This last-named candidature made little sense. Carnera had twice won on points against Levinsky (1931 and 1932) and a fight between Neusel, a middling German heavyweight, and the Italian champion would keep the American fight fans away from the Garden in droves. A match with the other German, Max Schmeling, a former – if disputed – world title holder, might possibly have generated some action at the box-office, but apart from the fact that the American Max, in his only fight in 1933, had beaten his German namesake by a technical knockout, Carnera had put his great foot down against a Schmeling challenge. The German had broken an undertaking to give Primo a crack at his title in 1931. He could now take his turn in the line.

The square-built, 24-year-old, 190 lb Steve Hamas made sense as a contender. He had knocked out Tommy Loughran, which Carnera had failed to do, and had only recently beaten Schmeling on points. But between Hamas and Baer as the next challenger, the Garden, which still had the champion under contract, saw a bigger gate potential in New York with the latter, what with Baer's appeal to women, his Jewish antecedents and the successful release of *The Prizefighter and the Lady*. With Carnera pulling the Italo-Americans, it offered a sweet scenario.

But Jack Dempsey, who still had Baer under contract, said he was willing to let the Garden promote such a match only if Baer received the same percentage of the gate as would go to Carnera. His argument was that Baer was just as big a drawing card as the Italian, 'if not bigger'. He was willing to release Baer from the contract binding him to the Yankee Stadium if that stood in the way of a title fight. His chief concern was to establish an American world heavyweight champion 'and thus revive interest in boxing'. But it would have to be a one-off deal with the Garden. There would be no question of extending their contract with Baer beyond 14 June, the date set for the fight.

Inevitably, Duffy retorted that he didn't care what percentage Baer got from the Garden; Carnera must be guaranteed considerably more than the 37½ per cent provided in the contract that bound him to the Garden until 30 September of that year, otherwise he would not fight under their auspices. In the event, the Duffy camp accepted the contracted percentage for Carnera and Dempsey dropped his absurd claim for parity with the titleholder; it was that or having to make way for another challenger to the title, with the loss of his own 37½ per cent rakeoff from Baer's 15 per cent of what promised to be an excellent gate.

Meanwhile, the Carnera management syndicate, now effectively headed by Duffy, Soresi and Friedman, were squabbling over their respective percentages, over the responsibility for the financial fiasco of the Loughran fight and the wisdom of accepting the Baer challenge. Soresi and Friedman had qualms about it but Duffy was all in favour. He needed money, urgently. The ending of Prohibition had put him out of the bootleg business, and under the new administration of Franklin Delano Roosevelt a whole corps of judges, both federal and district, were taking tougher stances against racketeers and tax-dodgers, as Al Capone had discovered. Like the legendary Chicago gang boss, the fun-loving and profligate Bill Duffy was in trouble over non-payment of income tax. In normal circumstances, he would have turned for help to his longstanding partner in crime, Owney Madden. But Madden was having trouble of his own. Since his release from Sing Sing on parole, two days after Carnera's defeat of Sharkey, he had become associated with a commercial concern contracted to supply coal to the municipal authorities of New York City. It had come to light that the supplier's method of measuring the weight of coal, delivered and signed for, differed fairly substantially from the actual weight reaching the civic depots. Some might have put the discrepancy down to innocent failings at the loading level. The city's prosecutors were calling it fraud, and seemed determined to make the charge stick.

A few months earlier, after being arrested, Bill Duffy had pleaded guilty to having failed to report a 1930 net income of $34,171.50 from fifteen bouts fought by Primo Carnera. Released on bail of $5,000, he had then been summoned to appear before the Federal Court in New York on 5 March 1934 to receive sentence from Judge William Bondy, but he had failed to show up. It seemed that another and more pliable judge had agreed to allow Duffy's sentencing to be deferred until after the Loughran fight in Miami, where Big Bill was expecting to raise the $2,207 owed on his 1934 earnings. Eight days after the fight, he had still failed to appear, but was reported by an assistant US Attorney to be on a Miami train heading for New York. Judge Bondy declared his bail forfeit and offered the advice: 'If he knows what's good for him, he'll be here at 10.30 in the morning.' He was, and was promptly sentenced to four months in the Federal House of Detention.

It meant that, instead of being in the champion's corner when he defended his title against Baer, Bill Duffy, together with millions of Americans, had to be content with listening to the exciting round-by-round commentary over the radio. And 'exciting' was no overstatement as far as a couple of elderly Pennsylvanians were concerned. Mr Edward Cassidy, a 72-year-old fight fan, suffered a fatal heart attack during the first round as he heard over the radio in his Holidaysburg home that the Man Mountain had been knocked off his feet. A few rounds later into the radio commentary, the same fate visited Mr Henry N. Geist at Big Run, near Punxutawney. A less dramatic but touching reaction was reported from London, where Emilia Tersini stayed up until the early hours of 15 June to follow the commentary on ticker-tape in a news room. As the fight progressed, hope alternated with despair on her face, and at the end of it she covered her face with her hands, wailing, 'Baer kept fouling him. Why didn't they disqualify him? I know Primo can beat him. I still believe in Primo!'

Primo was devastated by his defeat. There would be unstinting tributes in the morning newspapers to his courage in absorbing and fighting back against the battering by his challenger, but it would not lighten the shame he was suffering from the loss of his beautiful title. He wept uncontrollably in his dressing room after the fight. To those who sought to console him, all he could do was blurt out, 'I lose, don't you see! I lose da championship – dat's all!' And with a desperate grasping at straws: 'I not ask Donovan to stop eet. I not quit. I fight until I no more move, but I not geeve up.' In the opinion of James P. Dawson of the *New York Times*, 'He could have appealed to the referee without discredit to himself. He had gone further than anyone expected he would after those three knockdowns in the first. More, on none of those knockdowns did Carnera take advantage of the nine-second count to which he was entitled and which an experienced fighter would use. Maybe this hastened his downfall . . .'

It was that same pride, in spurning the count, that was now

tearing him apart. He had failed the leader of his nation, Benito Mussolini. He had failed the thousands of Italo-Americans who had made the pilgrimage to the Long Island Bowl and the millions of native Italians who would read of his defeat by a Californian playboy in the morning newspapers or who had already heard of it, as it was happening, over short-wave radio. He had failed every one of the 1,400 inhabitants of Sequals. And he had failed his family, especially his father, who had walked so proudly at his side through the village streets, just a few months ago.

He was spared, for the next few weeks at least, the unkindest cut of all, delivered – as it was to Caesar – by his own countrymen. This was the report of a special investigator sent to New York by the Italian Federation of Boxing, a report that would shock the Italian press and public by declaring that Carnera had lost to Baer 'under reasonably fair circumstances'. Up until them, few true Italians doubted that their idol, Primo, had been deprived of the title by a combination of bad luck and outrageous fouling. But here was an official report blaming Carnera's eleven downfalls in the ring to 'imprudent and mistaken strategy and disregard of the advice of his seconds'. And it went on: 'The irregularities [sic] committed by Baer during the fight were taken into account in the point calculation and the referee stopped the fight because he judged Carnera unable further to defend himself efficiently.' This, the report conceded, was to some extent due to 'a slight fracture of the right foot'. The Federation would accept the special investigator's report and would announce that Carnera had voluntarily resigned as heavyweight champion of Italy, 'thus opening the field for youth, in keeping with *il Duce*'s policy that no post in business, sport or any other field should be held so as to shut off unnecessarily the rising generation'.

For days, as he lay in bed nursing his torn ankle, the ex-champ continued to stare into a dark tunnel with just a faint glow of light at the end of it. There would be a return match. Not that the triumphant Baer was in a hurry to defend his newly won title; this would follow a series of elimination bouts between such contenders as Max Schmeling, Walter Neusel, Steve Hamas, Ray Impellittiere, Art Lasky and Tommy Loughran. However, Baer – and he had been quoted after the fight as saying it – he would be willing to give Carnera a return bout in September 'if there is enough public interest'. But a downcast Luigi Soresi was trying as gently as possible to advise his boxer against pinning much hope on the possibility. The myth of the all-powerful, indestructible Ambling Alp had been shattered and, with it, his awesome appeal to the fight fans. There was no way it could be restored by September. Primo must have known this, but he pretended otherwise. 'Because I slip in the first round and sprain my ankle, I lose da fight. But when I meet dat Max Baer again, I keel him and everyone will shout, "Viva Primo!" and will know again dat I am da real champion.'

Soresi had a more immediate reason for being downcast. The net gate for the title fight, after federal and state taxes, had been $361,337. Carnera's 37½ per cent of that came to $135,501. On the eve of the fight the Madison Square Garden Company had paid $88,000 (£17,600) into Carnera's bank account, but Emilia's lawyers had secured an injunction against any withdrawal of the money until her damages had been paid. Soresi was claiming he was owed precisely the amount of the Garden's deposit by his boxer and was appealing to the State Supreme Court. In the meantime, it was thin pickings for the loss of the world title, and it was time to think about putting the ex-champion back to work.

There were just a couple of problems. One was the difficulty, now, of fixing a match that would draw a big enough paying public. The other had to do with Carnera's state of mind, which could only be described as profoundly depressed. He was still insisting that Baer and the referee had, between them, stolen the fight: Baer by his constant fouling and Donovan by turning a blind eye to it. And it was even worse than that, the conspiracy to rob him of his beautiful title. Ten days after the fight, the *Sunday Express* published a strip of pictures taken from the film of the fight. A series of frames revealed an extraordinary and totally impermissible intervention by Donovan. Carnera is on

one knee and halfway through the ropes, his back half-turned to
Baer. Baer is over him with his fist drawn back and about to hit
him. The next frames showed Donovan grabbing Baer and
preventing the blow that would have disqualified the challenger
and left Carnera with the title. Most fight fans would be against
allowing such a foul to decide the outcome of a title fight; but
rules were rules and this was a particularly blatant example of
partisanship by a supposedly neutral official.

As the New York summer of 1934 cooled into the fall, Primo's
hopes of being able to redeem himself with a return bout were
fading. Baer was far too busy enjoying his reign as champion to
accept a title challenge from any quarter. Between Hollywood
parties and pleasure trips he was taking time out for a series of
lucrative four-round exhibitions againt non-ranking heavyweights while steering well clear of any commitment to put his
title on the line for at least a year. His one departure from this
easy routine with easy partners happened in Chicago, where he
was to give an exhibition with King Levinsky, whom Carnera
had beaten on points in 1931 and 1932. The first round passed
uneventfully enough, with Baer clowning as usual; but in the
second round the irritated Levinsky made the mistake of
abusing him, whereupon Baer stopped grinning and, with a
vicious hook, laid the 'Kingfish' out for the count for the first
time in his career.

For Carnera, it was out of the question to return to Italy until
the shame of his defeat had been expunged, one way or the
other. In the meantime he was becoming an all too easy prey to
the coyotes of both sexes who thrive on the grateful patronage of
fallen idols. In short, he was keeping bad company, drinking
and wenching too much for his health and his shallow purse.
Worse, he was telling anyone who cared to listen how disgusted
he was with prize-fighting and how he was thinking seriously of
giving up the game.

An invitation to fight Vittorio Campolo in Buenos Aires on 30
November came like rainfall in the Sahara to the Italian's
managers and seemingly even to Carnera himself. A second

victory over the Argentinian giant whom he had knocked out in 1931 would not bring redemption. But since his recent emergence from semi-retirement, Campolo had already beaten the Uruguayan champion, Mauro Caluso, and the giant Portuguese José Santa. He was almost as tall as Carnera, though about 30 lb lighter, and might have lasted much more than two rounds of that New York fight had he not angered the easygoing Primo by threatening to disgrace him in front of his expatriate *compatrioti* in Madison Square Garden. Interestingly enough, it was the presence in Buenos Aires of such a large colony of Italian immigrants that had persuaded the promoters to put the two giants together again in the ring. The Independiente Football Stadium, where the bout would take place, could hold 60,000 spectators. There would be a purse for Carnera of at least $18,000. There was just one snag: the winner would be expected to fight Paolino Uzcudun, now already on his way to Buenos Aires from Spain. If there was a *bête noire* among the succession of Primo's opponents, it was the husky 'Bull of the Pyrenees'. Knowing this, Soresi assured Carnera that a way could always be found to avoid a third meeting with the Basque, if only by insisting on terms unacceptable to Uzcudun's managers.

The fight with Campolo lasted the full twelve rounds, with a clear points win by Carnera. It proved nothing, except perhaps the lack of championship substance in both contestants. But the fans were pleased enough with the show and the promoters were furious when the follow-up bout with Uzcudun was scratched, after a wrangle between the respective managers over the percentages of a Carnera–Uzcudun gate.

Carnera had no wish to spend that Christmas in Italy, or to hang about in New York hoping for a return date with Baer. South American hospitality was lavish. The climate was excellent and the women obliging. After Christmas there would be a couple of exhibition bouts in the capital of neighbouring Uruguay, followed in quick succession by two prize-fights in Brazil: one against the negro Seal Harris in São Paulo, the other against Erwin Klaussner, an Estonian, in Rio de Janeiro. Neither of these opponents would have lasted more than a couple of rounds with the Carnera of six months earlier. In January 1935 they were in the ring with a huge, sun-bronzed Italian physically and temperamentally softened up by the Latin-American *dolce vita*, who took all of seven rounds to wear down the Negro to a standstill and six rounds to do the same to the Estonian.

But the tour had helped to lift the boxer out of his depression. It was time for him to get back to New York and into serious training while his managers went about setting up a series of bouts that would lead to a rematch with Max Baer.

9
Black Nemesis

Carnera's managers were in the hands of the Madison Square Garden Company, who had Carnera under contract for his next fight in the USA. And the NYSAC would have to approve the choice of opponent. A short cut to Baer would have been, first, a bout with Art Lasky, and then with the winner of a match in Hamburg between Max Schmeling and Steve Hamas, fixed for 11 March. Twenty-four-year-old Lasky, whom Carnera had beaten on points in the course of his 1932 juggernaut tour of the States, had since punched his way to contender status with a series of knockout victories and was ready and eager for a rematch with the Italian. Hamas, as noted in the preceding chapter, had already beaten Schmeling once on points and had shared contender status with Baer following Carnera's win of the heavyweight title.

But there would be no such short cut for Carnera. Instead, he was to fight the 24-year-old Ray Impellitiere, a relatively inexperienced Italian–American from upstate New York. Art Lasky would be matched against an Irish–American named James J. Braddock. The winners of these two bouts would then fight it out for the privilege of meeting either Schmeling or Hamas in a final elimination bout for a title fight against Baer.

In physical terms, Carnera *v*. Impellitiere was truly a battle of giants, the younger man being an inch taller and only a few pounds lighter than Primo. Between them, they weighed a quarter of a ton and made even Jack Dempsey, their referee, look like a cruiserweight. There were 19,000 spectators at the Garden's indoor arena in Manhattan, making it the largest indoor attendance for a fight in two years, and $44,953 was grossed at the gate. Carnera was a 4 to 1 favourite and the outcome, after an unexciting start, ceased to be in doubt from the sixth round onwards.

In top form, Primo dominated the fight, but was probably losing points for repeated low punching. Early in the ninth round, in seeming reaction to a low punch from Impellitiere, the ex-champion responded in kind, whereupon his opponent's manager, Harry Lenny, clambered through the ropes and demanded that Dempsey disqualify Carnera. The Manassa Mauler angrily ordered him out of the ring and promptly disqualified the enfeebled Impellitiere, giving the victory to Carnera by a technical knockout. It was an unsatisfactory decision, from someone who had no apparent reason for favouring the ex-champion. Dempsey would have been aware, of course, that Carnera's low punching up until the ninth round was not deliberate. The Italian had been confronting an opponent whose 'belt' was a little higher even than his own. On the other hand, it is possible that Dempsey was seizing the opportunity of denying Primo the prestige of a knockout victory. But a more likely explanation was that the veteran pugilist simply lost his short temper with Lenny for daring to tell him how to do his job.

This was a month during which the neat sequence of elimination bouts planned by the Garden's boxing supremo, James J. Johnson, started to go awry. Five days before the Impellitiere bout of 15 March, Max Schmeling had unexpectedly punched his way back into Adolf Hitler's good books with a knockout victory over Steve Hamas. And towards the end of that same month, another of the strongly favoured contenders bit the dust. Art Lasky needed just one good win to put him in line for a title fight. They matched him with a hungry Irish–American from Manhattan's 'Hell's Kitchen' district, James Braddock, who entered the ring with odds of 3 to 1 against him and outpointed Lasky over eleven of the fifteen rounds.

In principle, there were now three front runners for a title fight with Max Baer: Schmeling, Carnera and Braddock. And in principle they should have first fought it out among themselves. But since neither the German nor the Italian was willing to invite 'Cinderella Man' Braddock to the ball, the Garden rightly named him as the challenger for the title and set the bout for 13 June.

Up until 1933, Damon Runyan, together with two colleagues working for the Randolph Hearst newspapers, had been putting on fights at the Long Island Bowl and donating 10 per cent of the gates to Mrs Hearst's Free Milk Fund for Babies. The deal with the Madison Square Garden Company was ended that year when, according to one version, the Garden refused Mrs Hearst's request for a larger share of the boxing revenues. Another version had it that the cause of the split was the Garden's raising of its rents. Whatever the reason, the situation put the three influential journalists into cahoots with the 54-year-old Mike Jacobs, a former ticket hustler for the Garden's legendary George 'Tex' Rickard and now a fledgeling promoter on his own account. Both parties had a vested interest in ending the Garden's virtual monopoly of professional boxing, and they promptly achieved their purpose with a successful promotion at the Bronx Coliseum. Together, they then formed the Twentieth Century Sporting Club, the springboard from which, within a few years, Mike Jacobs himself came to dominate the New York prize-fighting scene.

Jacobs's first promotion for the club happened to be in the same year, 1934, when a 20-year-old amateur boxer from the slums of Detroit won the Golden Gloves heavyweight championship in Chicago. He was black and his name was Joe Louis Barrow. Later in that same year he fought as a professional for the first time, KO-ing his opponent halfway through the first round. By the end of the year he had dealt more or less as summarily with all eleven of the heavyweights put into the ring against him, including Stanley Poreda and Hans Birkie.

About this time, Mike Jacobs and company were looking to set
up some attractive promotions for the summer of 1935. Jacobs
already had a beady eye on the young black who was drawing the
fans to the Chicago Stadium; there was some promise here,
maybe even a future champion, given about five more years of
shrewd management. In the meantime, Baer was tied to the
Garden for his next title fight, which would be against Art
Lasky, after Lasky had taken care of the non-ranking fighter,
James J. Braddock.

Carnera's managers were becoming as anxious as Mike
Jacobs to make some money in June, the peak month for open-
air fights in New York. And if they were to get a title fight with
Baer later that year, Primo would have to pull off some
convincing victories against worthy opponents. Bill Duffy knew
about the hard-hitting young Detroit boxer and was thinking
about signing him up; but he was beaten to the puncher by
Jacobs, who put Louis under contract to the Twentieth Century
Sporting Club and set about fixing up a first fight in New York
for the promising newcomer. It did not take long for Jacobs and
Duffy to come to terms. With their two fighters on a bill
together, they were practically guaranteed a good gate. The
Stadium was close to the Harlem district. The blacks would turn
out in force for Louis and the Italians for Carnera. And the other
American fans would be drawn to this 'mixed' fight between the
races, something that Jacobs's one-time boss, the legendary Tex
Rickard of the Garden, had long opposed. The deal was settled
and signed in March, shortly after the Carnera–Impellitiere
bout. Carnera would get 35 per cent of the gate, Louis 18 per
cent.

Madison Square Garden, arch-rival of Twentieth Century,
reacted by declaring that the Italian had 'automatically'
disqualified himself from a return fight with Max Baer; but no
one took this seriously. Prize-fighting, to its promoters, is about
money; everything else, including loyalties, is incidental. And
prize-fighting is also prone to surprises. By 25 June, the date of
the Carnera–Louis match, the championship picture had
already undergone a dramatic change, with Art Lasky's

unexpected defeat by James Braddock and the latter's promotion to Number One challenger for the world title in a bout that was to take place at the Garden twelve days before the Carnera–Louis fight at the Yankee Stadium.

It was Baer's first defence of his title and, characteristically, he took his training less than seriously and could not resist clowning from the first bell. By the last bell, at the end of fifteen rounds, he had lost the title to Braddock, who gave him a lesson in straightforward unspectacular pugilism. The Carnera–Louis contest now took on even greater significance. Jim Braddock turned out to be one of the most popular of champions, but he was a plodding boxer, with little explosive power in his punches. Joe Louis had scored eighteen knockouts in the course of twenty-two undefeated fights. He would be giving away 70 lb to the giant Italian and could probably forget about a knockout victory over the bigger man. But if, using his superior skills and ringcraft, he could take the fight to a points win, only Baer should then stand between him and a challenge to Braddock. 'Should' was, of course, the key word; but the black Americans could now at least entertain the possibility – for the first time since the defeat of Jack Johnson in 1915 – of a young man of their race becoming heavyweight champion of the world.

They swarmed into New York from the mid-West and the cities of the south, augmenting the legions of their Manhattan brothers and sisters, thronging the streets of Harlem for days and nights before the fight, some with tickets bought at three times their face value, others with no hope of getting into the stadium but determined, anyway, to celebrate the 'Brown Bomber's' victory over the white Italian whose nation, under its fascist leader, was already being mobilized for a savage and unprovoked assault on the black population of Abyssinia.

Joe Louis, by his essential decency and dignity, would do more than any other black, with the possible exception of Martin Luther King, to bolster the pride and self-confidence of his people in the United States. But, unlike King, he hadn't a political bone in his body, as most of us found whenever we tried to draw him out on the subject of racialism in the United States.

But he was not above a mild quip at the giant Italian's expense, as when, at the weigh-in, after one look at his opponent's lower extremities, he murmured, 'With those feet, Primo sure kin cover a lotta grapes.'

With the knowledge that, whatever Madison Square Garden had to say about it, he was just one, or at the most two, victories short of a chance to regain the title, Carnera went into rigorous training for the fight. As Duffy saw it, the greatest danger would come from the young black boxer's incredibly swift and lethal hooks, delivered at close quarters and with crisp accuracy. Carnera would need to depend more than ever on his long left jab to keep Louis from working too close. The trouble was, Primo had so seldom had to go the full ten or fifteen rounds with his opponents that his arms tended to tire after half an hour's vigorous punching. To cope with this weakness, Duffy had four dollars' worth of nickels and dimes packed around the wrists inside the boxer's bandages for his sparring and bag work.

Joe Louis had no such problems; but being just one inch over six feet, he needed the experience of some really tall opponents. Accordingly, his trainer, Jack Blackburn, hired a trio of giants, all taller than Carnera, as sparring partners: Leonard Dixon, Roy 'Ace' Clark and Cecil Harris.

An estimated crowd of 64,000 – the biggest in eight years of New York prize-fights – was packed into the stadium by the time Joe Louis entered the ring, followed five minutes later by Primo Carnera. The black spectators, totally segregated from the white as was then the practice, acclaimed their champion with a roar that would have raised the roof, had there been one over the stadium. Among the ringside celebrities eyeing the panther-like movements of the 'Brown Bomber' were the US President's two sons, John and James Roosevelt, 'Fiorello' LaGuardia, Dempsey, Tunney, Baer and the new world champion, Jim Braddock.

Carnera's entry excited no comparable greeting from the Italo-Americans. For one thing, he was no longer their conquering hero. And there was another reason for their restraint: Benito Mussolini was making no bones about his

intention to invade and subjugate Abyssinia in defiance of the
League of Nations. The generations of Italian immigrants to the
United States, however proud they might be of their cultural
heritage, were split between those who were content to admire
(from afar) the fascist leader and those who saw him for what he
was: a preposterous and bellicose dictator whose actions could
alienate the Italo-Americans from their fellow-citizens in the
host country. There had been reports that Carnera was
determined to win because he 'owed one' to *il Duce*. Craven
though it might seem, there were plenty of ambivalent Italians
in the stadium that night ready to cheer him if he won and to
cheer Louis if the fight went the other way.

It began at 10.04pm and Carnera delivered the first blow, a
left to the body. In that same split second, as a lightning right
counter-punch from Louis snapped the giant Italian's head
back and opened a gash in his lip, Carnera would have realized
what he was up against. What he was up against was perhaps the
most efficient pugilistic machine ever transformed into human
shape. Joe Louis moved as if every part of his body enjoyed its
individual intelligence while responding smoothly and elegantly
to the super-intelligence screened by an otherwise totally
expressionless face. He wasted no punches. His powerful body
could weave and bob with the fluid grace of a lightweight. He
was a master of the feint; that sudden threat from a fist, or a
sway, or a look in the eye – sometimes all three at once – that
raised or lowered an opponent's guard and opened the way to a
hook as joined to the feint as the pain is to the sound of a
whiplash. Carnera tried hard during that first round to connect
with his straight left; Louis coolly ducked or slipped it and
moved in with crisp combination punches, testing rather than
sapping his opponent's strength. Meanwhile, the blood was
oozing from the Italian's lip, split because his seconds had
neglected to insert his gumshield at the opening of the round.

In his corner at the interval, an ashen-faced Carnera listened
and grunted as his lip was attended to and as Duffy spoke
urgently into his ear. Throughout the first round he had
adopted his usual stance, standing almost bolt upright as he led

with his left. He must try more of a crouch, using his massive arms (and elbows, if he could get away with it) to protect his chin and stomach while he sought an opening for his well-trained right-hand chop. It was sound enough advice, but against an artist like Louis it was irrelevant. He invited Carnera's right, slipped around it and landed his jarring one-two combinations at will, reopening the Italian's lip and bringing down upon Primo the boos of the spectators for using his great elbows to lessen the punishment.

Carnera came out fighting for rounds three and four, but apart from a glancing blow to Louis' chin, all his energy and skill had to be devoted to keeping the Brown Bomber at bay and clinching whenever he could. Even then, in the clinches, his usual advantage in weight failed to work with Louis. Carnera's surprise at this caused him to make his only remark to Louis during the fight. Joe later recalled, 'In the fifth, when I turned him around in a clinch, he said, "Oh, *I* should be doing that."'

By then, the Italian was in no state for doing anything but stay on his feet and absorb Louis' merciless blows, with only his courage and pride keeping him in the fight. There were more cuts in his lips now. The blood stained his chest, Louis' gloves and the floor of the ring. His left eye was grotesquely swollen. The end of the torment came in the sixth round. A series of hard rights to the chin put him down for a count of four. He staggered up, only to be floored again by lefts and rights, perfectly timed. On his feet again, with the referee, Arthur Donovan, anxiously eyeing him, he managed to mutter through his torn lips, 'Give eet to heem, give eet to heem,' whereupon Donovan immediately stopped the fight and raised Louis' arm in victory.

Unsurprisingly, the black section of the crowd erupted in wild jubilation. But from too many Italian throats came boos and catcalls aimed at the loser. And his own manager and second, Duffy, disgusted even the most hardboiled of ringsiders by bawling out his fighter, in their hearing, for 'a stupid performance'. One turns gratefully from such ignoble behaviour to the tribute paid to a brave loser, much later, by Joe Louis' own brother, deLeon Barrow: 'Carnera fought from bell to bell, and he didn't get no credit for it.'

The repercussions of Carnera's defeat were felt far beyond the Yankee Stadium. An obviously overwrought Professor Rayford W. Logan of Atlanta University declared, the following day, 'I'm afraid the defeat of Carnera last night will be interpreted as another insult to the Italian flag, which will permit Mussolini to assert again the necessity for Italy to annihilate Abyssinia.' Without going quite that far, official circles in Rome reacted sternly to the outcome of the fight. An order went out to all Italian editors from the Ministry of Popular Culture, responsible for control of press and propaganda: 'In no circumstances are you to publish any photograph of Primo Carnera knocked off his feet.'

There was worse to come. In more than one interview on his return to Italy just a few weeks after the fight, Primo spoke about how, during the second round of the fight, he suddenly began to feel weak. There was only one way he could account for it: in his corner, as one of his seconds passed a dripping sponge over his face and gaping mouth, he had smelled something 'strong and acid'.

Carnera was not by nature a liar. If he said the wet sponge smelled and tasted of something unusual, then it undoubtedly did. It might, though, have been a case of wilful self-deception. One of his seconds would have been treating the cut in his lip with the appropriate coagulant, and that could have accounted for the smell and taste appearing to come from the sponge. But how much more tempting, in his misery, to put it down to mischief of one kind or another. And how silly of him to hint at such in the interviews, when it was so obvious that in Joe Louis he had met one of boxing's greatest phenomena, someone who in fact went on to flatten Max Baer in four rounds, take the title from Jim Braddock and defend the crown from all comers for the next twelve years.

Fascist sporting circles in Italy were rightly infuriated and shamed by Carnera's *bêtise*. Members of the Italian Boxing Commission were at once flown to New York to look into all the circumstances of the fight. They reported to Rome that Carnera had been beaten fairly and that any charges of doping or threats by gangsters were absurd. Achille Starace promptly ordered the suspension of Carnera's passport and declared that he would not be permitted to fight the German heavyweight, Walter Neusel, in Amsterdam that September. Nor, for the present, would he be allowed to accept any other bouts in the United States. And an order was immediately issued to the Italian press, banning the publication of any more interviews about, or references to, the suspect sponge.

There were no compensating factors on the money front that year. In February, Carnera had finally lost a drawn-out and costly legal claim of £25,000 against Max Schmeling for breach of contract in failing to fulfil his pledge of a fight back in 1931. Now, as he went in retreat at Sequals, licking his wounds, his financial affairs were being put to intense and distressing scrutiny in New York's Supreme Court. On legal advice in London, Emilia Tersini had made a bid for her overdue breach-of-promise settlement by assigning her claim to a New York lawyer named Theodore J. Skratt. Skratt had won his application for an extension, to cover the Louis bout, of the already granted receivership against Carnera. He wanted to collect $15,000 from the $79,682 that Soresi, according to Skratt, had been paid on Carnera's behalf by the Yankee Stadium promoters of the Louis fight. In opposing this extension of the receivership, Soresi was saying that Carnera's share had been only $43,000 after tax contingency withheld by the promoters, and that he, Soresi, was still owed $88,000 for the Atlantic Beach property and the two Italian villas he had sold Carnera in May 1931.

Scratt reminded the court that when the Italian boxer was examined in the bankruptcy proceedings about those two Italian villas, he could not describe the colour of the villas nor say how many rooms they contained! And he contended that since the filing in 1933 of his bankruptcy petition, Carnera had earned more than $400,000 in the United States alone, leaving aside his earnings from the South American tour. Then came the allegation that most upset Carnera. There was a conspiracy, said Skratt, on the part of Luigi Soresi 'and others' to defraud not only the boxer's creditors but the boxer himself.

For Carnera, contemplating his pecuniary resources at that time, there must have seemed to be more than a grain of truth in Theodore J. Skratt's accusation. He was aware, since he had connived at it, that the 1,000-acre farm and two grand villas 'sold' to him by Soresi had, in Judge Schmuck's words, been a figment of the imagination and a device to prevent dunning creditors from getting their hands on his hard-won funds. Yet still, in his own words, he 'got no dough', not even an accounting of what had happened to the $400,000 he was supposed to have earned over the past two years.

John D. MacCullum has written* that Primo Carnera's professional prize-fighting bouts grossed more than $3,000,000 in purse money. No reliable figure was in fact ever published, even after Carnera's death, of his total earnings as a boxer, and the occasional estimates made during his career have to be treated with reserve, even with scepticism, if coming from one or another of his managers. They would as blithely exaggerate for publicity purposes as they would understate for the tax collectors. Research of all the relevant facts and fiction concerning the boxer's earnings leads to the conclusion that Mr McCallum's estimate was not far out, give or take a hundred thousand dollars either way. Such a figure will not seem impressive in the light of the vast sums earned by present-day heavyweight champions, until it is measured against the dollar's purchasing power in the early thirties, when a hotel room and bath could be had in Manhattan for $10 a week, an unfurnished apartment on Lexington Avenue for $40 a month, a man's suit for $15 and a restaurant meal for 65 cents. At the nation's average wages in 1935, Carnera would have had to work for 2,400 years to earn his $3,000,000, which in terms of the dollar's purchasing power in 1990 was the equivalent of $28,000,000.

There is also the fact that network and cable television, the

* Op. cit., p. 169.

major provider today of prize-fight purses, did not exist in the
early thirties. And any truly accurate assessment of his earnings
should include the cash payments made 'under the counter' for
exhibitions, other forms of public appearances, endorsements
and the like, especially during his twelve months as titleholder.
These payments would have been made directly to his managers
and it is unlikely that the boxer would have seen a penny of
them. But, all in all, and assuming his managers had left him
only 40 per cent of his earnings, he ought to have been able to
end his boxing career with more than the $7,000 he possessed on
his return to Italy in 1939, just before the outbreak of the
Second World War.

The brutal truth is that he never received anything like 40 per
cent of his earnings, from the day Sée and Dickson first put him
into the ring against Leon Sebillo. It would be an exaggeration
to say, as they did about Max Baer, that 113 per cent of his
earnings were owned by managers and outside investors. There
was no need for such overloading of ownership. In theory, after
contractual commissions to his American and European
managers, he would have been left with $42\frac{1}{2}$ per cent of his
purses. In practice, he would never have seen even 10 per cent.
His managers drew their commissions from his gross earnings,
before account was taken of their out-of-pocket expenses,
training costs, travel, legal fees, promotion expenses and the
myriad items involved in a ranking heavyweight's activities.
Carnera would have been *credited* with $42\frac{1}{2}$ per cent of whatever
net amount might be left in the kitty. But even this figure would
be shrunk by fictitious deductions. The end result was that he
was left with little more than pocket-money, but with the right
to borrow from his managers for such personal indulgences as
the monthly remittances of up to $400 to his mother and the
funds sent to Checu for the building of his villa. All such loans
would sooner or later have to be settled from his gross earnings.
The effect was to force the boxer, as from mid-1933, into
voluntary bankruptcy.

10
Squeezing the Lemon

It would have been sad enough if his need for money had been the sole incentive for Carnera's return to the ring four months after his crushing defeat by Joe Louis. Sadder still was his stubborn belief, cynically exploited by his venal managers, not only that he would win a rematch with the Brown Bomber but that he could go on from there to recapture the beautiful title he had lost so unluckily and unfairly in the ring with Max Baer. The best he might have hoped for, not unreasonably, would have been a return bout with Baer, who had lost his world title to the 'Cinderella Man', Jim Braddock, on points over fifteen rounds. Baer was already being written off as a top-ranker. He had been put into the ring against Louis while Carnera was in Italy recovering from the same experience. But unlike the Italian, who had fought six valiant rounds against Louis, the Californian playboy–pugilist had quit in the fourth round, squatting on the canvas while he listened to the referee's count. His performance – or lack of it – had earned him the disgust of his patron and chief second, Jack Dempsey, and the rest of the white spectators.

Almost two more years elapsed before Louis received the crown for which he was so obviously predestined; in the meanwhile, no one in his right mind would have given Carnera the faintest of chances of a successful return bout with the Brown Bomber. Duffy and Soresi were certainly under no illusion about this. They could still probably count on a reasonable turnout of customers drawn by the prospect of watching the Italian Goliath brought down by a series of American Davids. But first they had to get Primo back out of Italy.

It was during that September of 1935, while Carnera was licking his wounds in the ever-supportive ambience of Sequals, that Benito Mussolini launched his bombers, tanks and artillery against the north-east African kingdom of Abyssinia. In Rome, there was some talk at first of ordering Carnera to the front to boost the morale of the invading troops. But they were doing so well at the onset of the war against the naked, spear-carrying tribesmen that *il Duce*, who regarded boxing as 'an exquisitely fascist means of self-expression', was talked into letting Carnera have a crack at repairing his image by taking on Walter Neusel, the blond German heavyweight rated by some boxing critics as a possible successor to Max Schmeling. The match had the approval of the NYSAC and could therefore be staged at Madison Square Garden rather than in Amsterdam as had originally been planned by Jeff Dickson. Bill Duffy had hired a new trainer, Nick Florio, who was confident he could coach Primo to a win over the 209 lb Neusel. This might earn him a return bout with Louis and the chance of a challenge for the Braddock title. And if he lost against Neusel? Hell, the big bum could still pull punters into the ball parks for maybe another year or so. But Duffy and Florio were in fact counting on a win over Neusel. Spies in the opponent's camp had confirmed that the German's right eye was not yet fully healed from the damage done to it in a previous fight and that Neusel's sparring partners were under orders to go easy on that side of his face. Carnera's long stabbing left, as near maximum efficiency now as it would ever be, was just the tool for this particular job. And so it proved to be when, in the fourth round of the fight, Carnera scored a direct and powerful hit on the German's right eye. It was not a blow that would have brought the Italian victory in any normal circumstances, but it shook Neusel, who promptly abandoned the fight, fearful of permanent damage to the eye.

With only a few weeks of the year left before their human horn of plenty returned to Sequals for Christmas, Duffy and Soresi staged two more bouts, one against Ford Smith in Philadelphia, the other against George ('Big Boy') Brackley in Buffalo, NY. These were straight fights against non-ranking heavyweights, the first of whom stayed the distance but lost the decision, while the second was knocked out in the fourth round.

There was now renewed talk of an oft-mooted, but never realized encounter between Carnera and Schmeling, the winner to take on Louis. The snag, as always, was the lack of interest in a bout between two non-Americans, at least as far as the New York public and promoters were concerned. The prospects of such a match were further diminished before the end of the year when Paolino Uzcudun was sent bye-byes by Louis in four rounds, the first time the tough Basque had ever been knocked out. Five months earlier, in Berlin, Uzcudun had lost on points to Schmeling; therefore logic, international politics and Mike Jacob's self-interest demanded that his black protégé should be invited to eliminate the German from contention before throwing the gauntlet down to Braddock. But . . . 'international politics'? Involving the 'good nigger', Joe Louis, who was refusing to be drawn into even domestic political tensions? Whether he liked it or not, his colour had made him a role-player twice over. He had already wiped a smile off the face of Mussolini, the butcher of Abyssinian blacks. What could be more fitting, in 1936, than the victory of an American fighter – albeit a black one – over a German contender now back in favour with his racialist and anti-semitic Führer? The bout was fixed for 18 June 1936, which happened to be the date that Adolf Hitler put Heinrich Himmler, the leader of the SS, in control of Germany's entire national police force.

It would be a night as dramatic as any in the history of heavyweight boxing. No one had ever – or would ever – accuse Schmeling of arrogance or stupidity, which made all the more surprising his apparent conviction that he could beat the Brown Bomber and, by going on from there to challenge Braddock, become the first heavyweight ever to regain his world title. The fight took place at the Yankee Stadium, in the Bronx just north of Harlem, with Schmeling marked down for defeat by all the bookmakers and boxing critics. Instead, he pulled off one of the ring's greatest ever upsets. By the almost exclusive use of murderously accurate right hooks, crosses and slams to Louis' head, he kept the Bomber battling bravely but hopelessly to stay in the fight before being counted out in the twelfth round. It was the first time Joe Louis had ever been knocked out. He exacted a summary revenge for the humiliation two years later when, as world champion, he demolished Schmeling during the first round of their rematch.

Mike Jacobs had made a deal with Duffy months before the first Louis–Schmeling fight: if for any reason the German had to pull out of the fight, Primo would take his place in the ring. Slight as the chances were of this happening, Carnera was eager to believe that the Fates owed him such a break, and was equally convinced that it would bring him victory. 'Louis can punch, but I could see how my own punches really shook him,' he assured his Italian admirers before sailing for New York on 15 January. 'I know how to fix him in two rounds.'*

Primo could hardly have believed this, even if a crystal ball had revealed to him Max Schmeling's stunning victory, five months later, over the seemingly unstoppable Joe Louis. He was talking out of the battered pride of a dethroned champion, to an audience all too eager to have their misgivings put to rout. His managers, Duffy and Soresi, would have been under no illusion about his chances with Louis, either before or after the Schmeling fight; their immediate concern was to put him to work and to reap whatever profit might still be squeezed from the appearance of his name on a billboard.

His 1936 programme began on 6 March at Madison Square Garden against the Argentine, Isidoro Gastanaga, who was also under Luigi Soresi's management. Gastanaga had been scheduled to fight Louis in Havana three months earlier and had been catapulted into sports page headlines by the Cuban uproar

---

* Santini, op. cit., p. 156.

over Louis' decision to take on Uzcudun instead. The Argentinian turned out to be no match for Carnera and the referee stopped the fight in the fifth round to prevent further loss of blood from a cut over Gastanaga's right eye. Ten days later, in Philadelphia, Carnera was pounded into a third-round technical knockout by a young black heavyweight named Leroy Haynes, billed as the 'Black Shadow'. Haynes was 70 lb lighter and 6 in. shorter than his opponent and at the time was listed only 39th in *The Ring* rating of heavyweights. Facing a giant who had stood up to six rounds of scientific hammering from the Brown Bomber, he took with him into the ring that night a right-hand punch as good as Sharkey's and a black fighter's eagerness to storm the white racist ramparts of title contention.

If Bill Duffy was by now aware of what was happening biologically to Carnera, it makes all the more shameful his agreement to a return bout at Ebbet's Field eleven days later between Haynes and the bewildered and humiliated erstwhile world champion. It was the first major outdoor programme of the boxing season and it attracted a crowd of 20,000, curious to see if the comparatively unknown young black could repeat his performance in Philadelphia or if it had just been a flash in the pan.

It was anyone's fight up to the sixth round. Until then, Carnera had been boxing well, using his long left jabs effectively and scoring with some good hard rights to his opponent's head and body. Haynes was having trouble getting through the Italian's guard; but by the sixth round he was succeeding and over the next two rounds he dominated most of the fighting, with Carnera missing badly and tiring visibly. In the ninth round, after taking a right and a left to his body, the Italian was seen to reel and then turn and grope his way to the ropes where he supported himself while the referee stopped the fight in Haynes' favour. With his left side paralysed from waist to ankle, Carnera was supported by Duffy and Florio to his corner and then carried to the dressing room by six of the New York police department's finest.

Over the next three weeks the doctors came up with varying

diagnoses of his condition. His own doctor, Vincent Farrini, explained to the press at the Hotel Victoria that in the course of twisting and turning during the bout Primo had sprained a back muscle. The resultant swelling had exerted pressure against the sciatic nerve, causing the paralysis. No one who knew anything about a professional boxer's daily physical routine, made up substantially of 'twisting and turning', would have swallowed that story. The doctors at Columbus Hospital, where Carnera was a patient for the next three weeks, offered a graver and more specific diagnosis: the boxer's left kidney had been paralysed by vein damage and thrombosis of the paracentral branch of the front cerebral artery. But it still begged the question: why this vulnerability in a giant athlete, still on the right side of thirty, whose kidneys had suffered far greater pounding in the past, especially from Paolino Uzcudun and Max Baer, without such a drastic consequence?

The answer, whether or not it was realized at the time by Carnera and his managers, lay precisely in the abnormal physical dimensions that had earned the boxer his sobriquet of Man Mountain, with its continuing appeal to fight fans. Carnera's huge size was the result of an over-functioning in his youth of the pituitary gland, causing the long bones and soft tissues of his body to increase greatly up to the age at which growth normally ceases. The condition, clinically categorized as 'gigantism' is rarely inherited genetically. It produces the bulk, but by having to work so hard early in life the gland eventually becomes worked-out, slowing down the reflexes and dulling the muscles. And with the decay of the pituitary there is often a weakening of the adrenals, the glands controlling anger and energy. Carnera's future, though he refused at the time to accept it, no longer lay in boxing. With his bulk, he might make it as a wrestler. But Bill Duffy, who had no interest in the 'grunt and groan' game, promptly sold his management interest to Soresi at a discount and walked out of Primo's life. He also seems to have turned his back, at the age of 53, on the more colourful of his past activities, for little is reported about him in the public prints until the obituaries on his death on 25 May 1952 at the home of his daughter Mrs Winifred Jackson in Lynbrook, Long Island.

Duffy's old partner in crime, Owney Madden, had earlier sold out to Soresi, having lost interest in Carnera after his defeat by Baer. He had taken over The Riviera, a roadhouse on the Palisades, New Jersey, and hired the services, on a monthly retainer of $250, of a former US district attorney to deal with such nuisances as indictments for illegal gambling on Riviera premises and his relationship with the State Parole Board. On 14 June 1935, eleven days before the Carnera–Louis bout, it was announced in the *New York Times* that the State's long surveillance of its 'erstwhile No. 1 racketeer' had ended that day. Madden was now free of all police supervision and there would be a formal discharge from parole in a few weeks' time. He was still only 44 years old, but the onset of emphysema, coupled with a reluctance to renew his acquaintance with Sing Sing, obliged him to seek a less picaresque way of life. He now married his second wife, the daughter of a former postmaster of Hot Springs, Arizona. In this desert resort, kind to sufferers from lung disease, he lived in quiet retirement with only occasional trips to Manhattan to catch a prize fight at the Garden, together with old friends.

It was only through being in such company that his name continued to appear at intervals in the press. On 3 May 1940, Madden was leaving the Garden after a prize fight in the company of Bill Duffy, Marty Krompler and, as Captain Rothengast of the NYPD put it, 'two other hoodlums and killers'. The good captain admitted in court that it was his policy to take Krompler, a former lieutenant of 'Dutch' Schultz, into custody 'any time I see him around'. This time, it was in connection with a crime he was investigating, or so he said. After a night in the holding cells, the old buddies were freed to go their separate ways, there being no ground for keeping them in custody on the usual vagrancy charge. Madden hurried back to Hot Springs, and to a climate so benign that he was able to survive until 1965 before chronic emphysema did for him what the electric chair and a dozen gangland bullets had failed to do.

★

Carnera, leaning on a stick, returned to an Italy whose masters
were looking the other way, but to a native village that would
never fail to welcome its best-known son with warmth and,
when necessary, forgiveness. He needed money now for his
medical bills on top of everything else, and after a few weeks'
treatment at the thermal spa of Abano, thirty miles south of
Venice, he felt fit enough to take part in a few exhibition bouts
with Italian heavyweights before spending Christmas in
Sequals with his family. There were more exhibition bouts the
following year, more paid engagements as a referee of matches
up and down the country; and as the months went by with no
deterioration of his health, Carnera fell prey more and more to
the delusion that he could make a rewarding come-back as a
prize-fighter, settle all his debts and regain the respect of his
fellow-countrymen. He might even have indulged a fantasy
about winning the world title again, despite the fact that it now
belonged to Joe Louis following his knockout victory over Jim
Braddock in June of that year. In this pipe-dream he would have
been encouraged by a revival of interest in him by certain
promoters in Britain and Europe and, astonishingly, even in the
USA, or more precisely in Madison Square Garden, now
seriously crippled by the fact that the new heavyweight
champion remained contracted to the Garden's arch-rivals,
Mike Jacobs and the Twentieth Century Club.

Common sense dictated that he should prove himself, all over
again, in a European ring before even thinking about crossing
the Atlantic. A young British promoter, Benny Huntman, had
offered a couple of fights in London in October, with the
prospect afterwards of a match with the British heavyweight
champion, Tommy Farr. However, the British Boxing Board of
Control was withholding permission for any such bouts,
maintaining that the Italian ex-champion was medically unfit to
enter the ring. Benny Huntman was not standing for that. He
made an appointment, at his own expense, for Primo Carnera to
be examined by no less an authority than Lord Horder,
physician by royal appointment to King George VI. Primo's
arrival brought out crowds of his ever-supportive London fans

and made most of the front pages. It also brought out a couple of bowler-hatted sheriff's officers who arrested him while he and Huntman were reading the newspapers over breakfast next morning at the Savoy Hotel. The sheriffs were armed with a writ of attachment for non-payment of £124 in UK income tax.

While Carnera was taken to the sheriff's office in Chancery Lane, a lawyer hired by Huntman hurried to the Bankruptcy Court in nearby Carey Street where he filed a petition in bankruptcy on the boxer's behalf and applied to a judge in chambers for Carnera's release to keep his appointment that day with the King's physician. The Italian was escorted by the sheriffs to Lord Horder's consulting rooms in Harley Street. A few hours later, upon being released from custody, he was rushed to The Ring at Blackfriars where a crowd of Londoners and sports writers had been waiting all day to watch him demonstrate his fitness, working out with sparring partners. While the cameras flashed and the fans milled around him, he told the journalists, 'I think I owe no money when I come to England. I think all my income tax is paid. Now they say I still owe. I am flabbergast. No one understand when I say I pay before. I am very worry. I sit and I eat nothing since breakfast. It seem I always have worry. I come here to fight. Now I think everything is OK.'

Next day, at a quickly convened hearing in the Bankruptcy Buildings, an Assistant Official Receiver reported, for the benefit of creditors, that Carnera's petition showed liabilities of £4,324, made up of £124 for income tax and the £4,200 damages for breach of promise, a debt that had been assigned to a party in New York. There were no assets. Since his return, insolvent, to Italy from the United States the petitioner had earned £520 from exhibitions in Italy, all of which had gone on living expenses. And the bureaucrat, savouring this unexpected exposure to the spotlight of press coverage, could not resist the usual homily: 'A good many people have the idea that some professional boxers earn fabulous sums of money and are wealthy people. In this case, as in many others, these fabulous sums soon disappear and it is a matter of surprise to the man in the street to find that one who has recently been a boxing champion is absolutely devoid of assets.'

The case was left in the hands of the Official Receiver and Carnera was granted permission to leave the country on his undertaking to return whenever the court required. Like the timorous curate's egg, Lord Horder's finding, after a second examination, was bad only in part. The eminent doctor found no signs of paralysis but ordered the patient not to box for the next two months.

This would take Carnera to somewhere around the middle of December, and there would be no point in bucking Horder's edict since the British Boxing Board of Control was still refusing to license a fight. So, for a while anyway, Britain was out. Across the Channel in France, Jeff Dickson, after a few quick telephone calls, offered to match Carnera with Albert Di Meglio, the French army heavyweight champion, at the same Salle Wagram where Primo had made his professional début nine years earlier. The resourceful Dickson had secured the necessary release for Carnera from the Italian Boxing Federation ban on his fighting anywhere outside Italy. The bout would take place on 18 November, and although it would leave so little time for Carnera to get back into shape after a year and a half away from the ring, Dickson expressed total confidence in his one time protégé's ability to flatten Di Meglio and to go on from there to take the European title. Apart from his impresario's profit, Dickson was still on 10 per cent of Carnera's European earnings and he had set up the fight in cahoots with the boxer's new manager, Benny Huntman.

If there was ever the spectacle of a lamb being sent to the slaughter, it was on view at London's little airport of Croydon on 6 November as Huntman and his boxer emplaned for Paris. Over the ensuing days, Dickson warned that the ever-chauvinistic Paris fans would be with the French boxer from the start, even if he had not been 50 lb lighter and a head shorter than Carnera. Primo would be well advised not to antagonize the spectators by using his physical advantages in weight and reach too early in the bout. And he had better forget all those

cute practices he had learnt in America, such as wearing his
opponent down in the clinches and then hooking on the break,
out of sight of the referee.

In the event, it would probably have made little difference
had Carnera ignored these instructions. Booed from the
moment he stepped into the ring, jeered every time a Di Meglio
blow struck home, he moved as if his legs and arms were
weighted with lead. From the start, he absorbed the punching of
Di Meglio with a kind of rueful stoicism, much as John
Steinbeck's character, Lennie, accepted Curly's vicious on-
slaught in the film *Of Mice and Men*. In excessive obedience to
Dickson's instructions, he made a point of breaking cleanly
from the clinches at the first barked call from the referee, each
time incurring, without resistance, a flurry of opportunistic
blows from the Frenchman. It was almost as if, far from having
learnt nothing since his début in that same arena, he had
reverted to the ponderous musclebound young giant of the
fairground booths. So lacking in power and direction were his
punches that, when Di Meglio dodged one of his right swings,
and it finished up on the referee's chin, the official carried on as
if being unaware of having been struck. At the end of ten
rounds, Di Meglio was declared the winner on points and
Carnera, his nose swollen badly and with an ugly gash under his
left eye, was booed all the way to the dressing room.

Signor Mazzi, secretary-general of the Italian Boxing
Federation, had journeyed especially from Rome to watch
Carnera's performance. To the defeated boxer, in his dressing
room, he said, 'I am convinced you ought to have been awarded
the verdict. The only thing against you is lack of practice.' To
the Italian reporters, later, he declared: 'I shall report to the
president of the Federation in Rome tomorrow. It is not up to
me to decide what is to happen. I shall continue to discuss the
situation because there are many questions to be decided. We
must not forget that Primo had only eight days of training here
in Paris, a totally insufficient preparation after nearly two years
out of the ring. It was ridiculous to put him up against a fit and
tough opponent like Di Meglio without a proper period of

training. I shall of course have to take account, in my report, of Carnera's sad financial situation. In general, my opinion is that he could still give a good account of himself after a month's training, but he no longer has much of a future in international boxing.'*

Jeff Dickson was obviously of the same opinion. He cancelled a fight he had already arranged for 6 December and had nothing more to do with Carnera. Six years later, as a photographer with US Army Force Intelligence, the debonair and much-liked sports promoter was reported missing, presumed dead, after an operational flight.

Benny Huntman was not yet ready to desert his new-found client, not so long as he was capable of climbing, more or less unaided, into a prize-fight ring. Carnera had never fought in Hungary, a nation then on friendly terms with fascist Italy and Nazi Garmany and under the dictatorship of Admiral Horthy, a fan of boxing. A quick trip to Budapest secured the stadium and Horthy's blessing on a match between the famed Italian Man Mountain and . . . ?

Here, the accepted norms of international prize-fight manipulation make way for an almost surrealistic train of events. The Budapest encounter would be between Carnera and Bob Adams, a 242½ lb Englishman, and it would take place on 4 December. *Correction*, two days later: the encounter would be between Carnera and a French heavyweight named Forgeon. *Correction*: Forgeon had pulled out, for no expressed reason. The fight, now in three days' time, would be between the Man Mountain and the 'champion of Yugoslavia', Josef Zupan, who would weigh in at around 223 lb against Carnera's 253. The fight in fact took place in Budapest on 4 December and Primo Carnera won by a knockout in round two. *Correction*: the fight took place on 4 December and Josef Zupan won by a knockout in round two.

For some light, at least, on the mysterious going-on in Budapest, we must look to the distinguished journalist and

* Santini, op. cit., p. 166.

biographer, Aldo Santini.

'The *Gazzetta dello Sport* says that Carnera disposed of his opponent briskly with a right cross to the chin. The paper's correspondent, in his telephoned story from Budapest reported that the Italian boxer appeared to be in top physical condition. And there was no suggestion of mediocrity or cowardice on the part of the mysterious Zupan . . . Nat Fleischer, in *The Heavyweight Championship*, maintains not only that Zupan was Rumanian rather than Yugoslavian, but that it was Carnera who was knocked out in the second round. This gives rise to the suspicion that it was the Italian newspapers that reversed the actual result of the fight out of love of country – or rather fascism. Could it at least have been reported that crowds had queued up at the box office to pay homage to a glorious former world champion? Not at all. The event was a financial disaster and its organizers swiftly sought another and more attractive opponent for Carnera. With Primo's enthusiastic consent, a return bout against Di Meglio was set for 15 December. But, two days before the fight, the Italian Boxing Federation informed the international boxing authorities that it had banned Carnera from all boxing activities outside of Italy pending further orders. At the same time, the Ministry of Popular Culture "advised" the Italian press either to kill, or at least play down, all stories concerning Primo Carnera.'

From all of this, Aldo Santini draws an obvious conclusion: 'It seems that Nat Fleischer had it right: the Rumanian, or Yugoslavian, Josef Zupan did in fact knock out Carnera and the fascist press lied about the result. If the Friulano had in fact demolished the Rumano-Yugoslav in two rounds, why would the Italian Federation want to silence the press?*

There was no return bout with Di Meglio, despite Benny Huntman's assurances that it would go ahead with or without

* Santini, op. cit., pp. 167–8.

the Italian Federation's consent. On 13 December, Carnera collapsed in the lobby of his Budapest hotel, was rushed to the Park Sanatorium, diagnosed as suffering from haemorrhage of the kidneys and given blood transfusions. His condition was reported as serious but not life-threatening. The doctor's view was that the kidney condition was more likely caused by his abnormal size than by his fighting. 'As a boxer,' he added, 'he is dead. As a man, we hope to bring him around.'

But Benny Huntman, who had headed briskly back to London while Carnera was in hospital, had a different story. The boxer's kidney problem was the result of a blow suffered during training for a return bout with Di Meglio. His condition was not as serious as it had been reported. The doctor in charge was satisfied that Primo would be able to return to the ring and Benny had already set up several bouts in Egypt for January. Meanwhile, he was in London to raise money to pay for Carnera's hotel and hospital bills.

The bills were paid just in time for Primo to reach Sequals by Christmas Day, but they were not paid by Huntman. As a last act of caring management – or stricken conscience – Luigi Soresi had negotiated the unfreezing of the money impounded in Carnera's account by the bankruptcy court. The debt to Emilia Tersini had been paid, and after settling the lawyer's bill and recouping his own loans to Carnera, Soresi was able to cable a balance of £3,200 to his stricken ex-client, thus enabling him to clear his Budapest debts and make his way back home, if not with money to burn then not totally broke, either.

There had been better Christmases: good times when his motorcade had been cheered through the tree-lined streets of Sequals, with children running alongside crying, 'Primo! Primo!' and the boot of his car loaded with presents for his family and friends. There had been joyful parties in the splendid Villa Carnera on the Via Roma, with his mother reigning proudly over the women in the kitchen, his father holding forth to his cronies about the merits and demerits of his son's opponents; with Severino telling a rapt audience about the

wonders of the USA, and Secondo, just in from London, forced
to respond, laughing, to the demands of later-arriving guests for
a sight of his Anthony Eden black homburg, the headgear
favoured by the British Foreign Secretary, and therefore by
every male in Britain with pretensions to bourgeois respectability.

There had been no 'get well' messages to the Budapest clinic
from Benito Mussolini or Achille Starace; and again – as at
Christmas of 1936 – no courtesy visits from the region's
blackshirt chiefs, military or civilian. He was finished as a
symbol of Italian virility as far as the party propagandists were
concerned. To the people of Sequals he was still a hero and they
showed it with their smiles and salutes, as he passed them,
slowly skirting the main piazza on his way to the Bottegon and a
game of cards with the old friends of his youth. But this was a
different Primo: slower to bare his great teeth in the customary
smiles, refusing the proffered glasses of wine with a rueful
gesture to his stomach, shifting uneasily on the bench as his
huge face registered a spasm of pain. Whatever treatment the
doctors in the Budapest hospital had provided, it seemed to be
far from remedial. Or perhaps it was a case of Carnera's finally
ignoring their strictures about alcohol and joining too liberally
in the New Year's Eve festivities. Whatever the fault, after
collapsing in his villa within two weeks of the start of 1938, the
giant was rushed in an ambulance to a specialist clinic in Padua,
thirty-seven kilometres south-west of Venice, where he was
operated upon by the surgeon Doctor Fosiani for the removal of
his right kidney.

During the long convalescence that further depleted what
was left of his money, there would have been plenty of time for
Carnera to dwell on the probable cause of his affliction. Was it,
as the Budapest doctors believed, the inevitable consequence of
his enormous physique, or was it to do with the hammer blows
his body had taken in the ring, especially from Baer, Uzcudun
and Haynes? Either way, the fact remained that in that pre-
transplant era of medicine, his life now rested on the effective
functioning of just one kidney. Meanwhile, he would have to
find some means of paying his own way while continuing to

support his ageing parents. Prize-fighting was no longer an option. He could try professional wrestling, but there was little *afición* for the sport at that time in Italy, or even in the United States.

The solution – and the salvation – came with a visit to Sequals from the impresario of a touring variety show starring the popular Renato Rascel. Carnera was offered 50 per cent of the show's net box-office returns to appear each night in a sketch with Rascel and to spar, for one round only, with a volunteer from the audience. To a boxer who had made his theatrical début on the stage of the London Alhambra, who had sparred with a kangaroo in Atlantic City and starred in a Hollywood movie, the prospect held no terrors. He accepted at once and his début at Teatro del Parco in Milan's Giardino della Trienalle was a box-office and popular triumph. Fascist Italy might have written him off, but to the man and woman in the street he remained a living legend. He toured with the show throughout the rest of 1938. In November of that year he was invited to open a new shopping complex in the Italo-Yugoslav border town of Gorizia.

It was there that he met Giuseppina Kovacic. She was a 24-year-old Yugoslav and she lived in Santa Lucia d'Isonzo where her father, Giuseppe Kovacic, a former colonel in the Serbian army, held the office of mayor. She took the train every day to Gorizia, where she was employed as a clerk in the central post office, and according to one version it was at the railway station that Carnera spotted her upon his arrival for the opening of the shopping complex. He invited her to join him and his friends for a coffee after the ceremony. There and then he told the tall brown-haired beauty with the full lips and Slavic cheekbones that he had fallen in love with her and wanted to make her his wife.

In another version, Carnera first laid eyes on her across the counter of the Gorizia post office. 'Primo's schooling had been very limited. He was barely able to read and write. When he went to the post office, this young woman helped him to fill in a form. It was the start of their friendship.'*

Whatever the facts, Pina, as she was known to family and friends, was possibly amused but hardly flattered when Primo declared his intentions. She had no interest in boxing and could see nothing attractive in this human mastodon with the broken nose, enormous hands and peasant accent. And she happened to be already engaged to be married.

Carnera persisted. There were flowers and tender messages delivered to her home. Her father was infuriated; her *fidanzato* berated her to the point where she broke off the engagement. When his theatrical tour came to an end in the new year, Primo redoubled his attentions. He was rewarded in February with her 'I will' and in March with her 'I do' at their wedding in the parish church of Sequals. Pina's parents stayed away, but so many well-wishers converged on the village from near and far, crowding the narrow approach roads, that the bride's car was held up and delivered her an hour late to her nervous bridegroom.

The couple honeymooned in Capri, the Côte d'Azur, Spain and Paris. It was a voyage of mutual discovery by two people from different backgrounds, who had previously spent very little time alone together. And by all accounts, Pina came off the more disappointed from the exchange. She was the product of a bourgeois Yugoslav family, with a natural intelligence honed by formal education and with a cultivated taste in literature and music. Her husband's schooling had ended at elementary third grade. From there on, the one refining – and shortlived – influence in his life had come from Léon Sée: otherwise he had spent the years in the company of fairground barkers, an uncouth prize-fight fraternity and American hoodlums. Pina's misgivings can only have deepened when the couple returned from the honeymoon to settle down in Sequals. She was alienated from her own family by an unforgiving father, dependent for company upon friendly but unsophisticated villagers, denied the stimulation and distractions of her job at

* Umberto Branchini, *La Gazetta dello Sport*, 21 October, 1990.

the post office and married to someone who, however considerate and celebrated, was no longer a dependable breadwinner.

On all counts, it must have come as a great relief to both of them when Primo was offered a series of acting parts in films to be shot in Rome. With the exception of Alessandro Blasetti's *La Corona di Ferro*, these were not films of great merit and Carnera's roles had little award-winning potential. But there were no fewer than six of them from 1940, when Italy entered the war on Hitler's side, until 1942, two years before Rome was taken by the Allied armies.* It was a happy period for Pina and Primo. Their first child, Umberto, was born in Rome and it was there, in the Eternal City, that Pina set herself the task of furthering her husband's education with private tuition and her own guidance in reading and in appreciation of the arts. He was a responsive pupil, and by the time they settled down again in Sequals, at the beginning of 1943, they had more interests in common than Pina had ever believed possible.

No actor became rich from working in Italian movies during the war – and not so many afterwards, for that matter. Carnera's roles were mostly minor, and what with the costs of 'keeping face' as a living Italian legend and helping out his extended and indigent family, there was little left in the kitty by the time the Cinecitta operation was transferred from Rome to Venice.

The well-known Italian screenwriter, Luciano Vincenzoni, was then only a child, but he recalls how Carnera would from time to time bicycle almost two hundred miles from Sequals to Padua to visit his father, a dedicated fan of boxing and wrestling. Signor Vincenzoni was well-off and would make Carnera a gift of a kilo of precious lard and occasionally press a little money on him. What Luciano remembers most, however, was being perched on Carnera's knee and asked to peel an orange for him. 'There was no way those enormous hands could strip an orange without turning it into pulp.'

* *Vento di Milioni, La Nascita di Salome, Senzo Cielo, La Figlia del Corsario Verde, La Corona di Ferro* and *Harlem*.

In 1942 Pina had given birth to a second child, christened
Giovanna after her paternal grandmother. But with the invasion
of Sicily by the Allied armies in July 1943 and the consequent
signing of an armistice with the government of Marshal
Badoglio, martial law had been imposed by the Nazis upon the
civilian population of mainland Italy and Sequals remained
under German occupation until liberation in May 1945.

Primo's father, Sante, had died of a stroke in 1941, at the age
of 65. Secondo had already been interned on the Isle of Man
together with all the other 'unfriendly aliens' then living in
Britain, but his wife Marianna and their two little boys, Elvio
and Giovanni, had escaped internment by staying behind in
Italy. Severino was working in the mosaic business in New
Jersey when the war broke out in Europe and he was now
married to Mary Cola, a second generation Italian. It meant that
Primo was left to shoulder responsibility for his 65-year-old
mother, his wife, his sister-in-law and four children. And there
was a metaphorical burden – uniquely his – that would become
particularly troublesome as the Allied armies continued their
painful 'inching-up' campaign northwards. With the overthrow
of Mussolini, only the most fanatical of his followers continued
to have faith in the ultimate victory of the Axis powers.
Carnera's peacetime attitude to the blackshirt leadership had
been governed by a mixture of nationalist pride and pure
opportunism, as was almost certainly true of millions of his
fellow-countrymen. Disillusion would have begun with the rout
of Italy's North African armies and the surrender to Malta of
the Italian fleet. It would have been completed with the
imposition of Nazi military rule over its ally and by such
offences as quartering renegade Cossack battalions upon
northern towns and villages, including Sequals. In the
meantime, Carnera had a large family dependent upon him for
food and protection. The Germans had no reason for thinking
less of the former champion for having lost his title; to Carnera,
if this meant signing autographs for the soldiers and suffering
visits by their officers to his villa, he could live with that without
being suffocated by guilt as a collaborator.

But there were pitfalls, and Carnera stepped right into one when a message arrived for him from military headquarters in Venice. It was from Max Schmeling. He was now attached to a parachute regiment and the message spoke of how nice it would be if Primo and he could take a trip together in a gondola for old times' sake and drink to happier days.

Despite the legal action he had taken, and lost, against Schmeling back in 1935, Carnera felt no personal animosity towards the boxer and was touched by the invitation, with its offer of a military escort and hotel accommodation in Venice 'for as long as you would like to stay'. He should have smelt something fishy and found a means of excusing himself from making the trip, but he walked straight into the trap with his eyes wide open.

He had been exempted from military service on medical grounds and had been living quietly in his native village, out of the range of wartime propaganda machines. His arrival in Venice, into the warm embrace of Nazi Germany's most celebrated heavyweight champion, was too good an opportunity for demonstrating to the world, and to the Italians in particular, the vitality and durability of the Axis alliance, symbolized by this reunion of its two former world champions. As the German and fascist photographers crowded around the smiling, handshaking boxers, Carnera recognized the setup for what it really was. He managed to cut short his visit by pleading ill health, but the pictures with Doktor Goebbel's puppet would be a source of embarrassment when the time came to apply for a residence permit in the USA, although it was this nation that had already opened its side doors to some of Hitler's most odious henchman. And there would be something more menacing than embarrassment to face in Italy itself as the slow Allied advance continued and the Nazis began to be seriously harassed by partisans operating from mountain bases close to Sequals.

Various, and unreconcilable, accounts of Carnera's narrow escape from execution by the Italian partisans were in circulation after the war. The most circumstantial is given by

Robert Vattori,* who claims to have learnt the facts from one of the participants in the drama, Antonio Mora.

In the summer of 1944, with the Allied armies still battling hundreds of miles to the south of Sequals, an anonymous letter was delivered to the commander of a guerrilla group. It accused Primo Carnera of being a spy for the Germans. The commander, known only by the code name of 'Tom', found this hard to believe. He sent a courier to Sequals by night with a note for Antonio Mora who in turn aroused Carnera in his villa and told him he was to leave at once with the courier for the partisans' stronghold in the Meduna mountains. On arrival, Carnera was questioned closely by Tom. Satisfied, by the end of the interrogation, that the boxer was totally innocent of the charge, Tom shook hands with him and said he was free to go. Then he wrote two lines on a sheet of paper and gave it to Carnera, telling him to use it with discretion; it would protect him and his family from any further trouble with the partisans.

If Vattori's sources are to be believed, Carnera was later able to justify Tom's trust, one winter evening in Sequals, by saving the life of a partisan. The youth, weak from a bullet wound, had come down from the mountains in search of refuge in Sequals and was being helped to a safe house by a young girl of the village. Close to Carnera's house, the couple were challenged by two patrolling German soldiers, their suspicions aroused by the partisan's bandaged leg. Carnera happened to be passing by as the youth was being questioned. Catching an anguished glance from the girl and realizing quickly the cause of it, he approached the group and rested one of his great hands on the wounded boy's shoulder. 'My friend,' he growled in his deep voice, 'you should not be out in this cold. Get along to your house at once.'

It was the first time the soldiers, newly posted to the village, had seen this giant pugilist they had heard so much about. As they gaped up at him in awe, the young couple moved on into the shadows.

* Op. cit., pp. 119–22.

11
The Last Round

The war in Europe was over. Italy had been freed from both of its masters: Nazi Germany and Mussolini's blackshirts. Primo Carnera was nudging forty, missing one kidney, and broke. Except for simulating boxing during his variety tour with Renato Rascel, he had not put on the gloves since his collapse in Budapest, more than seven years before. He had been keeping as fit as his deficient wartime diet permitted, working out daily in his own private gym; but there had been no real sparring partners available in Sequals or the neighbouring towns, or the money to bring them in from further afield. Anxious as he was to earn money for the upkeep of his family, he knew he would have to forget his past glory and start again at the bottom of the prize-fight ladder, as he had in Paris, back in 1928. Any honest manager or competent trainer would have talked him out of a precipitate return to the ring. But professionally he was now on his own, and the wolf at the door of the Villa Carnera was drooling.

In July, Carnera accepted a bout in the nearby town of Udine with an unknown French–American named Michel Blevens, and finished him off in three rounds. Two months later, in Trieste, he knocked out a black American GI, Sam Gardner, in one round. In November, he took a bigger chance by challenging the European heavyweight champion, Luigi Musina, in Milan and was technically knocked out for his temerity in the seventh round. But it had brought him a decent pay packet and he agreed at once to a return bout, to be staged in Trieste in March of the following year. He was not fighting now for the European title: he was fighting for time and for some money in the bank. There were proposals from the United States for the Ambling Alp to start a new career in the increasingly popular spectator sport of freestyle, or 'all-in' wrestling, in which a man's loss of youth was less important than a fearsome physical appearance and some competence as an actor. He had the qualifications; what he needed was the money to get started in the States and to provide for his family until he could send for them to join him.

He lost on points to Musina in Trieste and lost again with their third encounter, two months later, in Gorizia. He was now finished as a boxer. The only question was: could he make it as a wrestler?

The auguries, according to a letter from the US promoter Harold Harris, were good. All-in wrestling had already become as big a craze as marathon dancing had been in the Twenties. With the advent of television it could only become bigger. Primo Carnera needed no introductory build-up as far as the American public was concerned. He had practised rudimentary wrestling in the French fairgrounds, and he knew far more about acting than most other newcomers to 'all-in'. Harris would stake him for one month's training before starting him out on a year's engagements across the States, wrestling or acting as guest referee of prize-fights.

He arrived at LaGuardia airport on 29 July 1946. One month later, he won convincingly against a wrestling star, Tommy O'Toole, and became literally an overnight star himself. Invitations now flowed in from every major city of the States and he fought with hardly a break over the next two years, sometimes as often as four times a week. And in this bizarre sport of 'grunt and groan', of choreographed mayhem, cultivated menace and bloodcurdling nomenclature, he was served, paradoxically, only by honest managers such as Harold Harris and the former middleweight wrestling champion, Joe

('Toots') Mondt. They took their agreed percentage – no more – from Carnera's purses, which were usually 20 per cent of the gate, and what was left after expenses and regular remittances to Pina went into Primo's bank account against the time when he could send for his family and make a nice new home for them in the United States.

His marriage, the children, the wartime deprivations and Pina's civilizing influence had made a more mature person out of the naïve hail-fellow-well-met giant so easily exploited during his career as a boxer. To his fundamental goodness was now added a deep sense of paternal responsibility and a love and respect for his wife greater than it had ever been. He wrote to her every day. If there was ever a delay in her own letters to him, he would send off a reply-paid cable and pester the local telegraph office for her response. And something of his evolved character seems to have informed his presence as a wrestler, for he came to be seen by the fans as the Good Giant, fouled and savaged by villainous opponents, many as big as or bigger than himself, who used every dirty trick in the book – gouges, rabbit punches, knees in the groin – but finally got their come-uppance, to the delight of the crowd, from a last-minute surge of Primo's power or the referee's belated disqualification.

In December 1947 he took up temporary residence in Mexico where a US consul helped him prepare an application to have his visitor's visa to the United States upgraded to an immigration visa. Re-entering the States at El Paso, he was subsequently granted resident status, a first stage towards full citizenship.

His earnings were now somewhere between $1,000 and $2,000 a week, the equivalent of between $8–16,000 today. It meant he would soon be ready to install his family in their first house in America. But his new-found fame and earnings inevitably attracted the same species of vulture that had hovered over him in the pre-war years. The difference now was that he had a wife he loved profoundly, who might find it difficult to believe that someone of her own sex could, out of greed, act unscrupulously towards another woman's husband.

The Italian journalist Umberto Branchini, writing in *La Gazzetta dello Sport* on 21 October 1990, recalled Carnera's concern to protect Pina from any such distressful experience. In 1947, Branchini was staying in New York when he received a phone call in the middle of the night from an agitated Carnera who had just arrived in the city from a wrestling engagement in Massachusetts. He didn't want to speak over the phone and he pleaded with Branchini to come at once to the Pennsylvania Hotel, where he was staying. It turned out to be a familiar enough story. After a bout, which he had won, Primo found himself in a restaurant frequented by dancers from a nearby music-hall. There was the usual buzz when Carnera walked in and he rose to the occasion by effortlessly lifting up one of the girls and planting her on a table. That was all there was to it – except that, next morning, observing bruises on her arms, the dancer went to a lawyer and, with the complicity of one of the restaurant's waiters, accused the giant Italian of an attempted sexual assault. Carnera left the state promptly, but had just heard that the lawyer and his client were pursuing him to New York. 'He was devastated', Branchini recalls, 'not by the thought of what it might cost him to settle the affair but out of fear that Pina would hear about it and think the worst.' Branchini found a lawyer who was able to clear up the bruises on the poor girl's arms by the magical application of a $1,000 bill.

Pina's feelings were spared. But Primo was greatly under-estimating his wife's ability to graduate from the simple values of Gorizia and Sequals to the harsh realities and the challenges of the New World. It was she who prompted the move to Southern California after her arrival in New York on 6 April 1948 and who negotiated the purchase, for $30,000, of their first house, on Genesee Avenue in Hollywood. It was a sound decision. In her view, New York City was no place to bring up their 9-year-old Umberto and 7-year-old Giovanna Maria. And there were other advantages to life on the West Coast. They would be living close to the major Hollywood studios, where Primo had already worked in two movies and would be available for further 'big guy' roles whenever the dates and the money suited him. The shrewd mind of the former post office clerk was also playing with the prospect of investing her husband's savings in the expanding communities of the San Fernando Valley. Meanwhile she made a point of vetting all contracts with promoters of wrestling in the States and abroad and became, effectively, his business manager.

Between 1949 and 1955, during breaks from wrestling, Carnera was featured in half a dozen major films. In Hollywood: *Mighty Joe Young*, with Terry Moore; *Casanova's Big Night*, with Bob Hope and Joan Fontaine; *Prince Valiant*, with James Mason, Janet Leigh and Robert Wagner; *On the Waterfront*, with Marlon Brando and Rod Steiger. In Rome: *Achilles's Heel* and *The Giant*. In London: *A Kid for Two Farthings*, with Diana Dors.

In 1956, Columbia Pictures released a movie – *The Harder They Fall* – that might as well have been entitled 'The Carnera Story' for whatever difference it offered between fiction and fact. It was based upon the novel by Budd Schulberg, with Humphrey Bogart playing his last film role as an out-of-work sports writer and Rod Steiger in the part of an unscrupulous New York boxing manager. Steiger's scouts have come across a giant would-be pugilist, 'Toro' Marino, and have persuaded his little Argentine manager, Señor Grandi, to allow Steiger to take the boxer under his wing, sharing management commissions. The awkward and musclebound Toro was earning a miserable living as a stonecutter before working as a strong man in a fairground, where the local boxing manager had discovered him. Toro arrives in New York with his manager and is put into training by Steiger, whose plan is to hype the giant to contender status by clever publicity – handled by Bogart – and a series of fixed fights, including (yes!) one in which an opponent, unwilling to take a dive, has rosin rubbed into his eyes between rounds. There follows a 'fictional' sequence on the death of one of Toro's opponents who had already, before fighting Toro, had his brain damaged in a bout with 'Buddy Brennan', played by (guess who!) Max Baer. And so the film reels on, incorporating only the most sordid elements in the real-life Duffy–Carnera relationship and presenting the Toro–Primo character as a pathetic half-wit who winds up physically battered and broke. The writer-producer, Philip Yordan, even went out of his way to introduce such gratuitous pointers to the real-life identity of Toro as the inclusion of the sign 'Hotel Victoria' on the façade of the building where Bogart pays a visit to the giant boxer.

This ought to have been an open-and-shut case for the award of punitive damages, since it would have been virtually impossible to find any follower of sport in the USA who would not immediately identify 'Toro' with Primo Carnera, to the detriment and ridicule of the real-life boxer. Although the producers had the nerve to refute the identification, it should have been a pushover for Primo's lawyers. But not in a Santa Monica court and not with a major Hollywood studio as defendant. In throwing out Carnera's suit against Columbia Pictures and Schulberg, with its claim for $1½ million, Judge Stanley Mosk declared: 'One who becomes a celebrity waives the right to privacy and does not regain it by changing his profession from boxer to wrestler.'

Carnera's temerity in taking legal action against a major studio meant that he would never again be employed in a Hollywood feature film production. His final roles as an actor were as Dr Frankenstein's monster in a 1957 NBC-TV version of the classic story and as a giant wrestler tackled by Steve Reeves in the Cinecittá version of *Hercules Unchained*.

As a wrestler, in movies and in the real world of prize-fights, Carnera probably showed more technical prowess than he had as a boxer, if only because he could use his weight and height more effectively against most opponents. And according to 'Tiger' Joe Robinson, a former world champion in the Cumberland and Westmoreland style of wrestling, he was not above using some of the all-in wrestlers' weapons, such as the elbow jolt or jab, to crack the ribs of a brute such as the German Kurt ('Gargantua') Zehr, a seven-footer weighing 700 lb. Robinson, who is now kept busy as an actor and trainer, with his own gym in Brighton, East Sussex, was cast as Carnera's wrestling opponent in the Carol Reed film *A Kid for Two*

Farthings, shot at Shepperton in 1954. He remembers Carnera with affection 'even though the blighter was getting every week, for two months, the same money they paid me for the whole shoot, namely £2,000. But Primo was a lovely fella. He always went out of his way to pick me up in his limo on the way to the studio. And once, when I happened to admire his overcoat, he presented me with a replica of it the next day.'

Wolf Mankowitz, who had written the screenplay from his novel of the same title, also had praise for the Italian, both for his good nature and the professional way he went about his work as an actor. 'The only problem we had with him was this outrageous accent, borne on the deepest voice in the business. I had to keep cutting or rewriting lines he just couldn't get his tongue around.'

But it was his career as an all-in wrestler that brought the money in and kept Carnera in steady employment all around the world until his retirement from the game. He fought in the bullrings of South America, throughout Europe and Great Britain, in Japan, the Philippines, India, Singapore and Australia. It was in Melbourne in 1957 that he made his bid for the all-in wrestling championship of the world by defeating the 350 lb reigning champion, a Hungarian billed worldwide simply as King Kong. At the time, there were almost as many 'world champions' as there were nations with *afición* for the relatively unregulated sport. But King Kong's title ranked high enough among them for Carnera to be able to claim, with some justification, that he was the only man who had ever held the world titles both for boxing and all-in wrestling.

Other former heavyweight pugilists had tried and failed to make the switch to wrestling, including some who had humbled Carnera in the boxing ring. The only British boxer ever to beat him, Larry Gains, was defeated by Carnera as a wrestler on the very day that the Italian's creditors in Britain were paid off, pound for pound. The following year, when Primo took on Max Baer in an exhibition bout of wrestling – the first time two former heavyweight champions had ever done so – the referee called it a draw. But to the relief of many, a bizarre scheme to match Carnera, as wrestler, against Joe Louis, as boxer, for the title 'champion fighter of the world' was abandoned.

Meanwhile, Primo's naturalization papers were being processed and he was made an American citizen on 28 August 1953, together with Pina and the two children. His mother, Giovanna, had died in 1947, after suffering from diabetes for several years. Severino, now a worker in mosaics, was married to the second generation Italian, Mary Cola, and settled in New Jersey with their two offspring, Joan and John Carnera. Secondo, on his release from British internment, had sent for his wife Marianna to join him in north London with 8-year-old Elvio and 5-year-old Giovanni. He, too, worked in the traditional mosaic craft before taking a job as general handyman in Soho's famous Genaro's restaurant and then as barman in the neighbouring Caves de France. The three brothers were thus separated by thousands of miles, reunited occasionally in Sequals or when the most famous of all Carneras found himself on the East Coast or in Britain for professional engagements.

Pina had adapted to emigration better than the other Carnera women. She was an all-encompassing wife, mother and business manager. She studied for, and was awarded, a Californian licence to act as an agent for the sale and rental of unfurnished properties, and made successive homes for the family in Hollywood, Glendale and Culver City. She indulged Primo's fancies, first to own a restaurant specializing in pasta dishes, which she set up on Pico Boulevard, close to the Twentieth Century-Fox studios, and then a liquor store on South Brand Boulevard, Glendale.

As his best friends might have put it, Carnera needed a liquor store like he needed an ulcer – an ulcer, indeed, as massive as the one that had to be dealt with by surgery in Udine in 1959, during one of his trips to Sequals. At times of stress he had often turned to drink; now, with everything going for him, instead of finding it easier to do without the booze, the opposite had become true. There were reasons for it. All-in wrestling, unlike boxing, did not depend upon trigger-quick reflexes and peak physical condition; it was part 'beef' and part histrionics. Nevertheless,

there was enough strain put on the contracting muscles and
enough hard knocks to be taken from the floor of the ring – and,
willy-nilly, from one's opponent – to justify a restorative shot of
alcohol after the bout . . . then, perhaps, another . . . And there
was something else. For long stretches of time, as he toured the
States and the world, Carnera was without the stabilizing
influence of family life and separated from a wife he had come to
love and respect more than any other woman in his life. When
abroad, he wrote to her every day. As a susceptible Italian male,
he could still be tempted by the various categories of female
already defined in chapter 6. The difference now, from his
bachelor days, lay precisely in the love he felt for Pina and his
concern that there should be no gossip, however false, linking
him romantically or purely sexually with any other woman.
Drinking and the practice of adultery might not be mutually
exclusive pastimes, but there are circumstances in which the
former can compensate for turning one's back on the latter.

Primo had long since retired from wrestling when he was taken
to the hospital in Los Angeles in a state of collapse. He was just
sixty years old. He had outlived his two younger brothers, by six
years in the case of Secondo, who had died of lung cancer, and
by two years in the case of Severino, a victim of leukaemia.
According to the doctors who, as Pina put it in March 1967,
'have brought him back from the dead', he was suffering from
two potentially terminal diseases: diabetes and cirrhosis of the
liver. It was their view that the diabetes had been inherited from
his mother. The cirrhosis was already too advanced to be
susceptible of cure, even though the patient had given up
drinking months earlier, following a series of internal
haemorrhages.

Pina managed to keep from Primo the worst of the doctors'
prognosis. She sold the liquor store to a friend of theirs, Vicente
Garofalo, made her husband as comfortable as she could in the
apartment they owned in Culver City and prepared herself and
the children, who were now in their twenties, for what was to
come. Umberto had finished his naval service and was studying

medicine at the University of Guadalajara, Mexico. Jean (baptized Giovanna Maria) had graduated from UCLA and was engaged to be married to a young engineer. Both were thoroughly American in their outlook and aspirations, with little nostalgia for the country of their birth. The same was now true of their mother, who had made the complete transition, in appearance, speech and manner, from the attractive young clerk in the post office at Gorizia to the very model of a chic West Coast matriarch.

With Primo, it was a different story. He had made his name in the United States of America, but at a bitter and irrecoverable cost in plundered earnings and squandered health. He had never felt completely at home, either as 'Da Preem' to the cigar-chomping Italo-Americans of Manhattan or as the gigantic wop ogled by his children's precocious Yankee playmates. He had not even, after all this time, managed to lose his heavy accent, as Pina had within her first two years in the States. The happiest times had been during his trips to Sequals in the good years of the Thirties; waking up in his beautiful villa, taking a stroll around the garden, exercising in his gym, meeting his old Friulano-speaking friends in the Bottegon, whose walls were covered with pictures of the most stirring event in the story of Sequals: Primo's title victory over Jack Sharkey on 29 June 1933.

His children, those two young Californians, had been properly educated, unlike himself, and were now out on their own. He was no longer able to have a glass of wine or *grappa* or to eat *a sà faim*, and he was incapable of moving from one room to the next without the unbreakable ebony walking stick Pina had found for him in some downtown Hollywood store. He knew, from looking in the mirror, that he was losing weight rapidly; how could it be otherwise when he could not hold down even a small plate of pasta? Perhaps in Sequals, with its clean air and mountain spring water, he could keep in there for a few more rounds . . .

With Pina in close attendance, Primo arrived at Rome's

Fiumicino airport on 20 May 1967. There was a crowd of friends, journalists, airport workers and ordinary members of the public waiting to greet Italy's living legend with the usual cries of 'Viva!' and a blaze of photographers' flashlights. But when the last of the passengers had left the plane and Carnera, leaning on his stick, appeared at the exit door, there was a corporate intake of breath followed by stunned silence. The sunken eyes and cheeks, the dark suit hanging on the skeletal frame, wasted already by 80 lb – this was a cruel and grotesque travesty of the Friuli giant who had straddled the world of boxing and wrestling to become a symbol of strength and virility to his people. The silence persisted until, in the words of eyewitness Nantas Salvaloggio, quoted by Santini, the ex-champion, acting from long habit, raised his great hand in the victory gesture of a prize-fighter. But it was a shaky movement, the action of a tired and dreadfully sick old man. At this point, a veteran and threadbare pugilist in the crowd broke the silence with a loud cry of 'Viva Primo! Viva Carnera!' It was followed by hesitant, ragged applause.

After an overnight rest in Rome, Pina put Primo aboard a sleeping-car train direct to Udine. On every station platform along the way, little crowds of people were gathered, as if by bush telegraph, to salute the homecoming giant. He remained prostrate on his bunk, moved by their 'Viva's but unable to respond. At Udine, a forewarned specialist in liver disease met the Carneras and accompanied them in a limousine to their home in Sequals, where he examined Primo and confirmed the Los Angeles doctors' finding of terminal cirrhosis.

For the next five weeks, Primo was kept alive by drugs and intravenous feeding. As his condition worsened, Pina sent for the children, but only Giovanna Maria arrived. Umberto could not make it; he was taking his medical exams. On 19 June, the same parish priest, Giuseppe Dalla Pozza, who had married Primo and Pina twenty-eight years earlier, performed the last rites over the dying man, and on that same day, exactly thirty-four years after he took the world heavyweight boxing championship from Jack Sharkey, Primo Carnera lost his last fight.

*

They came in their thousands to the funeral in Sequals, not just from the surrounding towns and villages but from all over Italy. And if they could not get there, they sent floral tributes and telegrams by the hundred: from the USA, Great Britain, France, Germany and South America; from old prize-fighters and glamorous movie stars; from two exiled monarchs, Edward of the House of Windsor, who had hosted him in London after the fight with Franz Diener, and Umberto of the House of Savoy, after whom Primo had named his first child. And the tributes came also from those ordinary boxing fans to whom Paul Gallico's words, back in 1930, were addressed: 'The coming of Carnera is a major event . . . the embodiment of the strange and unusual yet elemental qualities . . . [the] material for folklore.'

Epilogue

In May 1976, the village of Sequals, lying on the broad plain between the river Tagliamento and the sub-alpine Meduna mountains, was largely destroyed by an earthquake. Thanks in great part to the energy and resourcefulness of its mayor, Giacomo Bortuzzo, it has since been restored to the well-loved home of its thousand-odd inhabitants, including those native sons and daughters who, like Carnera, left it in their youth and have since returned to spend the rest of their days in its benign ambience.

One such former emigrant, Dante Bortoli, recalls how, as a young man working in Birmingham, England, he once watched Primo 'doing his stuff' in an exhibition bout. His father, Oreste Bortoli, used to drink with the giant in his favourite bar, Il Bottegon, on the Via Gian Domenico Facchina. It is upon such associations, a quarter of a century after Carnera's death, that a man's status in the community might rest. For as another repatriated emigrant, Adelico Galante, put it to the present author: 'If Sequals exists, it's because of Carnera.' An over-statement, of course. And yet, on closer acquaintance with the village, perhaps not all that fanciful . . .

In the barroom of Il Bottegon, where photographs of the boxer compete with pictures of that other major event in the history of Sequals, the 1976 earthquake, a boxing shoe once worn on Primo's right foot, and of almost absurd proportions, sits on an accessible shelf, offering itself, as it were, for inspection by any in need of proof that a true giant had passed that way.

The municipal headquarters of Sequals stands in a side street off the main *piazza*, Cesarina Pellarin. Inside the entrance, the first object to catch the eye from its dais on the right is a bronze bust of Primo Carnera.

From the *municipio*, it is a minute's walk back across the square, for a drink at the village's central bar, Al Cret (The Rock, in Friulano). Here, under a painting in colour measuring 48 x 48 inches, of Carnera, is the inscription, *Sei Sempre Vivo* (You are Living Still).

On the same side of the square, a few houses up, is the entrance to the Sala Somsi, housing a collection, mounted on forty panels, of photographs, press cuttings and posters assembled during Carnera's career by Gino Argentin, a citizen of Cordenone. On 27 June every year since 1983, half a century after Carnera won the world heavyweight title, the Sala Somsi and the main square outside become the venue for the Carnera Trophy, a programme of boxing matches. These are for the purpose of finding the best heavyweight from eight amateur clubs of northern Italy, those of Rimini, Rovigo, Trissino, Gorizia, Trieste, Piove di Sacco, Montfalcone and Pordenone. Earlier in the day, the contestants will have placed a wreath on the Carnera family tomb in the cemetery close by the Via Roma entrance to Sequals. The lofty tomb takes the form of a triangular Doric pediment supported by two pillars. Centred in the space between the pillars is a lifesize bronze bust of Primo, resting on a plinth bearing the inscription:

PRIMO CARNERA
1906–1967
Campione del Mundo
di Pugilato

On either side, inscribed on tablets, are the names and dates of his deceased father, mother and two brothers. The most recent inscription reads: Giuseppina Kovacic, vedova [widow] di Primo Carnera. The year of Pina's burial was 1980, when her coffin was transported from Los Angeles, in accordance with her wishes, to lie beside that of her husband. Its inclusion in the family tomb was an act of magnanimity at the time by her husband's blood relatives who had built the costly sepulchre after Primo's burial, without a financial contribution from his widow. This, however, was less a cause of ill-feeling between the family and Pina than her action over the villa at Number 10, Via Roma, that Primo had built out of such of his earnings as a boxer that he was able to save from the greedy grasp of his managers. After his death the villa became, of course, the property of his widow, who had no intention, however, of taking up residence in Sequals. This being also the case with Pina's two children, she decided to put the villa on the market.

The people of Sequals were outraged that she could do such a thing with the home that had given Primo so much pleasure and to which he had always planned to retire. The mayor of Sequals willingly accepted the duty of raising enough money, by public subscription and with the help of the Carnera family, to buy the villa and turn it into a museum to the memory of the community's most famous son. A fund was set up, but while it was still short of the figure set by Pina a firm offer was made by a businessman, Signor Micoli Amatildio, who was not a native of Sequals. His offer was promptly accepted by the widow.

At the time of writing, the house remains the private residence of the Amatildio family, retaining its name of Villa Carnera. It survived the 1976 earthquake without structural damage and its interior and gardens are maintained in superb condition by the owner. To their credit, the Amatildios have never exploited the commercial possibilities attached to ownership of the property. Visits are not invited, but genuine interest can usually be satisfied through the good offices of Mayor Bortuzzo. It was he who arranged with one of the beautiful and courteous Amatildio daughters for the present author to make a tour of the house and the private gymnasium built on to it: a particular object of pride to Primo Carnera.

To step inside the gymnasium is to be confronted from the opposite wall by a life-sized cutout of the boxer, stripped for action, with gloves raised and massive shoulders hunched. The punch-bag still hangs from the ceiling. The four pillars of the full-sized ring remain bolted to the floor, but the ropes have gone. Upon request, you may be handed the great ebony walking stick used by the stricken Primo towards the end of his life; just to take its weight is to understand how, even in sickness, the Man Mountain was still someone apart from the ordinary run of men.

So the little Italian village knows how to honour a man who brought it fame, however fleeting, and to some, perhaps, paltry. But the one memento that Carnera himself would have chosen, above all others, to symbolize his achievement and to be on display after his death is lying in a safe deposit box in the Banco di Verona at the town of Spilimbergo, just a few miles to the south of Sequals. This is the bejewelled belt presented to him when he became the twelfth member of the exclusive company of gloved world heavyweight boxing champions. Only his son, Doctor Umberto Carnera, can authorize its release and entrust it to those who still honour the memory of his father.

It is said that, among the older inhabitants of Sequals, there are those who believe that, until this is done, another earthquake could be caused by a risen Man Mountain making his way to Spilimbergo.

Primo Carnera's Ring Record

Year	Date	Venue	Opponent	Won	Lost
1928	12 September	Paris	Leon Sebillo	KO–2	
	25 September	Paris	Joe Thomas	KO–3	
	30 October	Paris	Luigi Regirello	TKO–4	
	25 November	Milan	Epifanio Islas	Pts–10	
	1 December	Paris	Constant Barrick	KO–3	
1929	18 January	Berlin	Ernst Rosemann	Pts–5	
	28 April	Leipzig	Franz Diener		Disq. 1
	22 May	Paris	Moise Bouquillon	TKO–3	
	30 May	Paris	Marcel Nilles	Pts–10	
	26 June	Paris	Jack Humbeeck	TKO–6	
	14 August	San Sebastian	José Lete	Pts–10	
	25 August	Marseilles	Joe Thomas	KO–4	
	30 August	Dieppe	Nicolaieff	KO–1	
	18 September	Paris	Herman Jaspers	KO–3	
	17 October	London	Jack Stanley	KO–1	
	18 November	London	Young Stribling	Foul–4	
	7 December	Paris	Young Stribling		Foul–7
	17 December	London	Franz Diener	TKO–6	
1930	24 January	New York	'Big Boy' Peterson	KO–1	
	31 January	Chicago	Elzar Rioux	KO–1	
	6 February	Newark, NJ	Bill Owens	KO–2	
	11 February	St Louis	Buster Martin	KO–2	
	12 February	Memphis	Jim Sigman	KO–1	
	17 February	Oklahoma City	Johann Erickson	KO–2	
	24 February	New Orleans	Farmer Lodge	KO–2	

Year	Date	Venue	Opponent	Won	Lost
1930	3 March	Philadelphia	Roy 'Ace' Clark	KO–6	
	11 March	Fort Worth	Sully Montgomery	KO–2	
	17 March	St Louis	Chuck Wiggins	TKO–2	
	20 March	Jacksonville	Franz Zavita	KO–1	
	26 March	Kansas City	George Trafton	KO–1	
	29 March	Denver	Jack McAuliffe	KO–1	
	7 April	Los Angeles	Neil Clisby	KO–2	
	14 April	Oakland, Cal	Leon Chevalier	TKO–6	
	22 April	Portland, Ore	Sam Baker	KO–1	
	5 June	Detroit	K. O. Christner	KO–4	
	23 June	Philadelphia	George Godfrey	Foul–5	
	17 July	Omaha	Bearcat Wright	KO–4	
	29 July	Cleveland	George Cook	KO–2	
	30 August	Atlantic City	Riccardo Bertazzolo	TKO–3	
	8 September	Newark, NJ	Pat McCarthy	KO–2	
	18 September	Chicago	Jack Gross	KO–4	
	7 October	Boston	Jim Maloney		Pts–10
	30 November	Barcelona	Paolini Uzcudun	Pts–10	
	19 December	London	Reggie Meen	TKO–2	
1931	15 March	Miami	Jim Maloney	Pts–10	
	15 June	New York	Pat Redmond	KO–1	
	26 June	Buffalo	Umberto Torriani	KO–2	
	30 June	Toronto	Bud Gorman	KO–2	
	24 July	Rochester	Knute Hansen	KO–1	
	4 August	Newark, NJ	Roberto Roberti	KO–3	
	6 August	Wilmington	Armando de Carlos	KO–2	
	12 October	New York	Jack Sharkey		Pts–15
	19 November	Chicago	King Levinsky	Pts–10	
	17 November	New York	Vittorio Campolo	KO–2	
1932	25 January	Paris	Moise Bouquillon	TKO–2	
	5 February	Berlin	Ernst Guering	TKO–5	
	29 February	Paris	Pierre Charles	Pts–10	
	23 March	London	George Cook	KO–4	
	7 April	London	Don McCorkindale	Pts–10	
	29 April	Paris	Maurice Griselle	TKO–10	
	15 May	Milan	Hans Schoenrath	TKO–4	
	30 May	London	Larry Gains		Pts–10
	20 July	New York	Jack Gross	TKO–7	
	28 July	New York	Jerry Pavilec	TKO–3	
	2 August	New York	Hans Birkie	Pts–10	

Year	Date	Venue	Opponent	Won	Lost
1932	16 August	Newark, NJ	Stanley Poreda		Pts–10
	19 August	New York	Jack Gagnon	KO–1	
	1 September	São Paulo	Art Lasky	Pts–10	
	7 October	Tampa, Flo	Ted Sandwina	KO–4	
	15 October	Camden	Gene Stanton	KO–6	
	17 October	Louisville	Jack Taylor	KO–2	
	4 November	Boston	Len Kennedy	KO–3	
	18 November	New York	José Santa	TKO–6	
	2 December	St Louis	John Schwake	TKO–7	
	9 December	Chicago	King Levinsky	Pts–10	
	13 December	Grand Rapids	'Big Boy' Peterson	TKO–2	
	16 December	Omaha	K. O. Christner	KO–4	
	19 December	Galveston	Jimmy Merriot	KO–1	
	30 December	Dallas	Jack Spence	KO–1	
1933	10 February	New York	Ernie Schaaf	KO–13	
	29 June	Long Island	Jack Sharkey	KO–6	
	22 October	Rome	Paolino Uzcudun	Pts–15	
1934	1 March	Miami	Tommy Loughran	Pts–15	
	14 June	New York	Max Baer		TKO–11
	30 November	Buenos Aires	Vittorio Campola	Pts–12	
1935	13 January	São Paulo	Cecil Harris	KO–7	
	22 January	Rio de Janeiro	Erwin Klausner	TKO–6	
	15 March	New York	Ray Impellittiere	TKO–9	
	25 June	New York	Joe Louis		TKO–6
	1 November	New York	Walter Neusel	TKO–4	
	24 November	Philadelphia	Ford Smith	Pts–10	
	9 December	Buffalo	George Brackley	KO–4	
1936	6 March	New York	Isidoro Gastanaga	TKO–5	
	16 March	Philadelphia	Leroy Haynes		TKO–3
	27 May	New York	Leroy Haynes		TKO–9
1937	18 November	Paris	Albert di Meglio		Pts–10
	4 December	Budapest	Josef Zupan	? (see p. 173)	
1945	22 July	Udine	Michel Blevens	KO–3	
	25 September	Trieste	Sam Gardner	KO–1	
	21 November	Milan	Luigi Musina		TKO–7

Year	Date	Venue	Opponent	Won	Lost
1946	19 March	Trieste	Luigi Musina		TKO–8
	12 May	Gorizia	Luigi Musina		TKO–8

Primo Carnera had 101 prize-fights during his twelve fighting years. He won 71 by knockouts or stoppages, 16 by points decisions and 2 by fouls. He lost 5 by knockouts, 5 by points and 1 by a foul.

Since the statistics vary widely according to their source, the following represent the *lowest* figures drawn from data published during the boxer's career.

Height	6 ft 5¾ in	Forearm	16 in
Weight	260 lb	Fist	14¾ in
Neck	20 in	Wrist	9½ in
Chest	48–54 in	Reach	81¼ in
Waist	38 in	Thigh	30 in
Biceps	18½ in	Ankle	11½ in

Appendix

Literal extract from *Le Mystère Carnera* the book by Carnera's manager Léon Sée, giving Sée's own listing of Carnera's fights from 1928–31.*

1928	Léon Sebillo	KO2	Combat arrangé	
	Joe Thomas	KO3	,,	,,
	L. Reggirello	KO4	,,	,,
	Epifanio Islas	V.10	,,	,,
1929	Marcel Nilles	KO3	,,	,,
	Jack Humbeeck	KO6	,,	,,
	Joe Thomas	KO4	,,	,,
	Barrick	KO4	,,	,,
	Nicolaieff	KO1	,,	,,
	Franz Diener	P.1	,,	sincère
			(disqualifié)	
	Moïse Bouquillon	V.10	,,	,,
	Young Stribling	V.4 (faute)	,,	arrangé
	Franz Diener	KO6	,,	sincère
	Young Stribling	P.7 (faute)	,,	arrangé
1930	Big Boy Peterson	KO1	,,	,,
	Elzar Rioux	KO1	,,	,,
	Cowboy Owens	KO2	,,	,,
	Buster Martin	KO2	,,	,,
	Jim Sigman	KO1	,,	,,
	Erickson	KO2	,,	,,
	Farmer Lodge	KO2	,,	,,
	Ace Clark	KO6	Cas douteux	

	Sully Montgomery	KO2	Combat arrangé
	Chuck Wiggins	KO2	” ”
	Frank Zavita	KO1	” ”
	George Trafton	KO1	” ”
	J. McAuliffe	KO1	” ”
	Neil Clisby	KO2	” ”
	Léon Chevalier	KO6	” sincère (disqualifié)
	K. O. Christner	KO4	” arrangé
	George Godfrey	V.4 (faute)	” sincère (disqualifié)
1930	Bearcat Wright	KO4	Combat arrangé
	George Cook	KO2	” sincère
	Bertazzollo	KO3	” ”
	McCarthy	KO2	” arrangé
	Jack Gross	KO4	” ”
	Jim Maloney	P.10	” sincère (déc. volée)
	Paolino [Uzcudun]	V.10	” ”
	Reggie Meen	KO2	” ”
1931	Jim Maloney	V.10	Combat sincère
	Pat Redmond	KO1	” ”
	Umb Torriani	KO2	” arrangé
	Bud Gorman	KO2	” ”
	Knut Hansen	KO1	” sincère (pas payé)
	Rob. Roberti	KO3	” ”
	De Carlos	KO1	” ”
	Jack Sharkey	P.15	” ”
	King Levinsky	V.10	” ” (arrêtés)
	Campolo	KO2	” ”

* *Arrangé*	Fixed fight
Sincère	Honest fight
Cas douteux	Doubtful case
Faute	Foul

Bibliography

Barrow, Joe Louis jnr, *Joe Louis, the Brown Bomber*, London, 1988
Fleischer, Nathaniel, *The Heavyweight Championship*, New York, 1961
Mihalache, George, *Primo Carnera*, Bucharest, 1975
Oats, Joyce Carol, *On Boxing*, New York, 1987
Sammons, Jeffrey T., *Beyond the Ring, The Role of Boxing in American Society*,
    University of Illinois Press, 1988
Santini, Aldo, *Carnera: l'Uomo Piu Forte del Mondo*, Milan, 1984
Sée, Léon, *Le Mystère Carnera*, Paris, 1934
Sugar, Burt Randolph, *Ring Record Book & Encyclopedia*, New York, 1981
Vattori, Roberto, *Primo Carnera: Campione Senza Tempo*, Udine, 1987

Index